# The Rehabber's Handbook



an all-inclusive how-to
for professionals and novices

## Bob Anderson

Krittergitters Publishing
Wills Point, Texas

*The Wildlife Rehabber's Handbook*


ISBN: 978-164008496-4

Printed in the United States of America

First Printing

Book design by Lee Lewis Walsh, Words Plus Design, www.wordsplusdesign.com

For more information or to order additional books, please contact:
Krittergitters Publishing
320 VZCR 3219
Wills Point, Texas 75169
U.S.A.
1-903-865-1013
www.krittergitters.com

# Contents

# Foreword

After more than forty years of rescuing and rehabilitating wild animals, we have come across a huge number of people who show an interest in this kind of work. Hundreds of people around the U.S. spend countless hours volunteering at wildlife centers and rehabilitation facilities because they want to help the animals. Generally, these people are eager to get involved, but know very little about the technical side of animal care. We have also come across a number of people who want to try rehabilitation for themselves. These folks also seldom have the training to take on the role of an animal care specialist. In addition, there are those who, while hunting, fishing or simply visiting their backyard, find a creature in distress and want to help it. Unfortunately, they have no idea what to do.

Some seasoned rehabilitators oppose non-professionals doing rehab work. They argue that, without the proper knowledge, these people will do more harm than good. Our opinion is that people are going to try to rehabilitate, regardless. We believe that the more information you can provide to these folks, the better their chances of avoiding harm — to themselves and to the animals.

We have therefore produced this book to be an all-inclusive "how-to" reference for both professional and novice rehabilitators. It will assist the reader with many procedures and aspects of animal care and, if followed, will greatly reduce any harm that might be caused by the lack of technical training.

Many of the animals that come in for rehabilitation are suffering from illnesses or injuries that require the attention of a licensed veterinarian. However, finding a vet that will work on wild animals can be difficult. We've learned that the best way to get a veterinarian's help is to visit all of your local vets prior to needing their help. Explain your rehab program and discuss the needs you anticipate; for example, if you intend to specialize in deer rescue, mention that. It has been our experience that you are more likely to get a vet on board if they know that no major time commitment on their part is involved. Also, a discussion of fees can help make your case.

Please keep in mind that there are many ways to complete a task and there are many different viewpoints on any topic. The information provided in this book is the result of our personal experience and informed opinions.

There are five members of the family Cervidae in the United States: white-tailed deer, elk, moose, caribou, and mule deer (see next page).

## Deer at a Glance

| | |
|---|---|
| Gestation period | 196 days |
| Weight at birth | 5 to 10 pounds |
| Formula | Multi-milk® |
| Frequency of feeding babies | 5x/day |
| Weaned | 11 to 12 weeks |
| Reproduction | Once per year, in mid to late spring |
| Litter Size | 1 to 3 fawns |
| Adult weight | 100 to 200 pounds |
| Hibernation | No |
| Natural foods | Acorns, grasses, leaves, corn, berries, twigs, fruits, nuts |
| Normal temperature | 101.1°F |

# Chapter One

# Deer

## Introduction

There are five members of the family Cervidae in the United States: white-tailed deer, mule deer, caribou, elk, and moose. These are some of the most beautiful and majestic animals in North America. Although almost everything in this chapter can be applied to all five species, it focuses on white-tailed deer.

Although gentle and dainty looking, white-tailed deer are very strong and can be extremely dangerous to handle.

Several years ago, an e-mail letter started circulating about one man's attempt to forgo hunting and simply catch him a deer. This has become an urban legend and provides a useful cautionary tale of a good idea gone terribly wrong. The author is unknown.

> *I had this idea that I was going to rope a deer, put it in a stall, feed it up on corn for a couple of weeks, then kill it and eat it. The first step in this adventure was getting a deer. I figured that, since they congregate at my cattle feeder and do not seem to have much fear of me when we are there (a bold one will sometimes come right up and sniff at the bags of feed while I am in the back of the truck not four feet away), it should not be difficult to rope one, get*

*up to it and toss a bag over its head (to calm it down), then hog-tie it and transport it home.*

*I filled the cattle feeder then hid down at the end with my rope. The cattle, having seen the roping thing before, stayed well back. They were not having any of it. After about twenty minutes, my deer showed up — three of them. I picked out a likely looking one, stepped out from the end of the feeder, and threw my rope around its neck. The deer just stood there and stared at me. I wrapped the rope around my waist and twisted the end so I would have a good hold. The deer still just stood and stared at me, but by now I could tell it was mildly concerned about the whole rope situation. I took a step towards it; it took a step away. I put a little tension on the rope and then received an education.*

*The first thing that I learned is that, while a deer may just stand there looking at you funny while you rope it, they are spurred to action when you start pulling on that rope. That deer EXPLODED!*

*The second thing I learned is that pound for pound, a deer is a LOT stronger than a cow or a colt. A cow or a colt in that weight range I could fight down with a rope and with some dignity. A deer — no chance. That thing ran and bucked and twisted and pulled. There was no controlling it and certainly no getting close to it.*

*As it jerked me off my feet and started dragging me across the ground, it occurred to me that having a deer on a rope was not nearly as good an idea as I had originally imagined.*

*The only upside is that they do not have as much stamina as many other animals. A brief ten minutes later, it was tired and not nearly as quick to jerk me off my feet and drag me when I finally managed to get up. It took me a few minutes to realize this, since I was mostly blinded by the blood flowing out of the big gash in my head.*

*At that point, I had lost my taste for corn-fed venison. I just wanted to get that devil creature off the end of that rope. But I fig-*

*ured if I just let it go with the rope hanging around its neck, it would likely get hung up and die slowly and painfully somewhere. At the time, there was no love at all between me and that deer. At that moment, I hated the thing, and I would venture a guess that the feeling was mutual.*

*Despite the gash in my head and the several large knots where I had cleverly arrested the deer's momentum by bracing my head against various large rocks as it dragged me across the ground, I could still think clearly enough to recognize that there was a small chance that I shared some tiny amount of responsibility for the situation we were in, so I didn't want the deer to suffer a slow death. So I managed to get it lined up in between my truck and the feeder — a little trap I had set beforehand, kind of like a squeeze chute. I got it to back in there and I started moving up so I could get my rope back.*

*Did you know that deer bite? They do! I never in a million years would have thought that a deer would bite somebody, especially me, so I was very surprised when I reached up there to grab that rope and the deer grabbed hold of my wrist. Now, when a deer bites you, it is not like being bit by a horse where they just bite you and then let go. A deer bites you and shakes its head — almost like a pit bull. They bite HARD and it hurts.*

*The proper thing to do when a deer bites you is probably to freeze and draw back slowly. I tried screaming and shaking instead. My method was ineffective. It seems like the deer was biting and shaking for several minutes, but it was likely only several seconds. Being smarter than a deer (though you may be questioning that claim by now) I finally tricked it. While I kept it busy tearing the bejesus out of my right arm, I reached up with my left hand and pulled that rope loose.*

*That was when I got my next lesson in deer behavior for the day. Deer will strike at you with their front feet. They rear up on their back feet and strike right about head and shoulder level, and their hooves are surprisingly sharp. I learned a long time ago that when an animal — like a horse — strikes at you with its hooves and you can't get away easily, the best thing to do is try to make a loud noise and make an aggressive move towards the animal. This will usually cause it to back down a bit so you can escape. But this was not a horse. This was a deer, so obviously such trickery would not work. In the course of a millisecond, I devised a different strategy. I screamed like a little girl and tried to turn and run.*

*The reason I had always been told NOT to turn and run from a horse that paws at you is that there is a good chance that it will hit you in the back of the head. Deer may not be so different from horses after all — besides being twice as strong and three times as evil — because the second I turned to run, it hit me right in the back of the head and knocked me down.*

*I also learned that when a deer paws at you and knocks you down, it does not immediately leave. I suspect it does not recognize that the danger has passed. What they do instead is paw your back and jump up and down on you while you are lying there crying and covering your head. I finally managed to crawl under the truck and the deer went away.*

*Now I know why, when people go deer hunting, they bring a rifle with a scope so that they can be somewhat equal to the prey.*

Whether this story is fact or fiction, we begin with it to make an important point: if you are going to handle deer, you are going to have to be very careful not to get hurt.

White-tailed deer are the smallest members of the North American deer family. Males (bucks) range from 100 to 300 pounds, while females (does) range from 75 to 200 pounds. The average length of a full-grown buck is approximately 6 to 7 feet, while females are somewhat smaller.

The white-tailed deer's coat will change with the seasons, from reddish brown in the spring and summer when vegetation is growing to grayish brown in the winter. This helps the deer stay camouflaged year-round. This change in color happens quickly, usually in one to two weeks. They have patches of white fur around their eyes, muzzle, and throat, as well as on their underbelly and under their tail. When a white-tailed deer is startled, it will raise its tail, exposing the white underside. This signal serves as a warning for other deer and gives the white-tailed deer its name.

Males lose their antlers each spring.

Only males have antlers, which they lose each year in the spring, usually in March and April, and rapidly regrow them immediately after loss. Some subspecies of white-tailed deer will grow antlers at a rate of one inch per day. The new antlers will initially grow in covered in hair-like tissue called velvet. During the summer months the bucks will rub the velvet off, leaving hard bonelike antlers. Bucks without branching antlers are often called spikes. Length and branching of antlers is determined by nutrition, age, and genetics. Healthy well-fed deer can have eight-point branching antlers as yearlings (1.5 years old). The number of points and the length or thickness of the antlers is a general indication of age, but cannot be relied upon definitively. Better indications of age are the length of the snout and the color of the coat, with older deer tending to have longer snouts and grayer coats.

White-tailed deer have relatively small home ranges, usually only one square mile or less. They gather into same-sex groups, or herds, to graze throughout the summer. Bucks will use this time to prepare for mating, also known as rut, which begins in early September. During this time, bucks will fight each other to claim the right to mate with does in the area. Females enter rut in October or November. Females

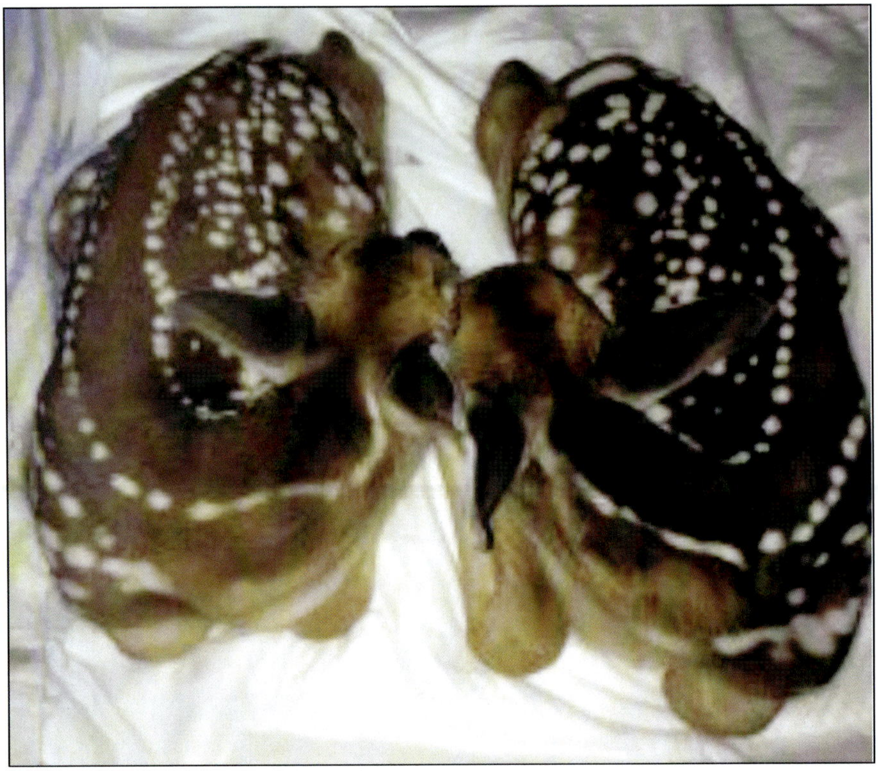

Every baby has its own unique set of spots.

may be as young as six months when they reach sexual maturity, but the average age of maturity is eighteen months. Males are also generally sexually mature at eighteen months.

Does give birth to one to three spotted fawns in mid to late spring, usually in May or June. They are very protective of their newborn fawns, only leaving them for short intervals to graze for food. When the mother is absent, the fawn will lie motionless on the forest floor, camouflaged from predators. Fawns are typically weaned at four to six months, but usually stay with the mother until she has another newborn. Fawns lose their spots during the first summer. Male fawns tend to be slightly larger and heavier than females.

During the mating season, adult male deer become very aggressive and dangerous as they compete for the opportunity to breed females. Sparring among males determines a dominance hierarchy and bucks will use their antlers to fight with each other during the rut. The sound of antlers clashing can attract does who are in heat. Bucks attempt to copulate with as many females as possible, losing physical condition in the process, since they rarely eat or rest during the rut. Many factors determine how intense the "rutting season" will be; air temperature is a major one. Any time the temperature rises above 40°F, the males do much less traveling looking for females, else they will be subject to overheating or dehydrating. The general geographical trend is for the rut to be shorter in duration at increased latitudes. Another factor in the strength of rutting activity is competition. If numerous males are in a particular area, then they compete more for the females. If fewer males or more females are present, then the selection process will not need to be as competitive.

The white-tailed deer is an herbivore with a diverse diet; they have been known to graze on more than 600 different plants. They love to eat acorns, vegetables, grasses, leaves, crops like soybeans and corn, hay, berries, twigs, fungi, fruit, nuts, bark, and clover. Foraging mainly occurs at dawn and dusk. This is when they are most active, making them neither nocturnal nor diurnal, but crepuscular.

The white-tailed deer is a ruminant, which means it has a four-chambered stomach. Each chamber has a different and specific function that allows the deer to eat a variety of different food, digesting it at a later time in a safe area of cover. The stomach hosts a complex set of microbes that changes as the deer's diet changes through the seasons. This specialized stomach allows them to eat some things humans cannot, such as toxic mushrooms and poison ivy.

They also have specialized teeth: sharp incisors for biting through vegetation, and big molars for grinding it up when they chew.

Natural predators of white-tailed deer include wolves, cougars, American alligators, and humans. Many predators frequently pick out easily caught young but can and do take healthy adults of any size. Bobcats, Canada lynx, bears, wolverines, and packs of coyotes usually prey mainly on fawns. Bears may sometimes attack adult deer, while lynxes, coyotes, and wolverines are most likely to take adult deer when the ungulates are weakened by harsh winter weather. Records exist of American crows attempting to prey on white-tailed deer fawns by pecking around their face and eyes, though no accounts of success are given. Occasionally, both golden and bald eagles may capture deer fawns with their talons. Few wild predators can afford to be picky and any will readily consume deer as carrion; many scavengers also rely on deer as carrion, including New World vultures, raptors, and foxes.

White-tailed deer typically respond to the presence of potential predators by breathing heavily (also called blowing) and fleeing. When they blow, the sound alerts other deer in the area. As they run, the flash of their white tails warns other deer. This especially serves to warn fawns when their mother is alarmed. Most natural predators of white-tailed deer hunt by ambush, although canids may engage in an extended chase, hoping to exhaust the prey. Felids typically try to suffocate the deer by biting the throat. Cougars and jaguars will initially knock the deer off balance with their powerful forelegs, whereas the smaller bobcats and lynxes will jump astride the deer to deliver a killing bite. In the case of canids and wolverines, the predators bite at the limbs and flanks, hobbling the deer, until they can reach vital organs and kill it through loss of blood. Bears, which usually target fawns, often simply knock down the prey and then start eating it while it is still alive. Alligators snatch deer as they try to drink from or cross bodies of water, grabbing them with their powerful jaws and dragging them into the water to drown.

Bobcats, still fairly widespread, usually only exploit deer as prey when smaller prey is scarce. In areas where they are heavily hunted by humans, deer run from people almost immediately, and are quite wary even where not heavily hunted. In most areas where hunting may occur, deer seem to develop an acute sense of time of day and a fondness for hunter-free metro parks and golf courses. Deer can run faster than their predators and have been recorded at speeds of 50 miles per hour; this ranks them amongst the fastest of all cervids. They can swim at speeds up to 13 miles per hour, and can jump 9 feet high and at distances of up to 33 feet. If frightened, the deer will hop in a zigzag pattern with its tail straight up. When shot at, the white-tailed deer will run at high speeds with its tail down. If the deer feels extremely threatened, however, it may charge the person or predator causing the threat, using its antlers or, if none are present, its head to fight off the threat.

## Common Causes of Injury

Deer are interesting animals and like most species they have some idiosyncrasies. For example, mother deer spend very little time with their young. To avoid attracting predators, moms will hide their babies in deep grass or brush and leave them alone for hours at a time while she forages for food. Shortly after birth, the momma deer will nudge the baby with its nose until the newborn falls down. Once down, the baby stays without any movement. The baby will not get up on its own unless mom comes to get it. It is cited in the literature that baby deer are one of the few animals in nature that do not emit any odor that can be detected by predators. Combined with the ability to stay perfectly still, this means that baby deer are very safe without mom hanging around. They can stay so still and remain so well hidden that most people could walk within a few inches of them without detecting them.

When it's time for baby to be fed, mom will never approach the exact spot where the baby is hiding, preventing predator detection. Mom will survey the area and, when she determines that the area is safe, she will give out with a barking sound that summons the baby to her. Once junior is fed, she will knock it down again and go on her way. This pattern will last for several weeks before the baby is finally allowed to tag along with the herd. On several occasions we have seen momma deer leave the baby for more than twenty-four hours at a time.

Baby deer can hide like no other animal.

This natural instinct of "duck and hide" is effective for keeping baby deer out of harm's way. But unfortunately it presents its own set of hazards. Because the fawn stays so still and will not run when discovered, it becomes easy prey for tractors, mowers, dogs, and humans. When a hiding deer is run over by a motorized vehicle or farm equipment, it will usually suffer major injury or death. Many deer will break or lose multiple legs in these types of accidents and will need to be put down.

Each year, more than 1.5 million deer are hit by automobiles in the United States. These collisions are hard to prevent because usually the deer comes out at sunset or sunrise when visibility is poor. Few people give much thought to hitting a deer because it is such a random event that most people think will never happen to them. When it does occur, most people don't know what to do.

There are two considerations to a car-deer collision. The first is the reporting obligation of the driver. Unfortunately, there is no standard protocol for reporting deer collisions. Many of these incidents occur in rural areas where it's not clear who to report the incident to. Each jurisdiction has its own protocols for reporting auto accidents. Some require reporting all auto accidents, others only require reporting accidents with property damage, and others set limits on damage levels and reporting. Complicating this is the fact that wildlife is managed by the state. Thus each state has its own set of rules and requirements concerning both reporting and disposition of the deer.

So what should you do? To cover yourself from possible legal issues, you should report the incident the same as you would any crash. Call 911 and report the incident and ask the 911 operator what you should do. If you want to harvest the animal for food, tell the operator of your wishes and let them tell you the state requirements. Be prepared to wait for a responding authority on the scene if requested to do so. You should also remember to contact your insurance company if you will be filing a claim.

The second consideration has to do with the deer. Although they seldom survive a collision, occasionally their injuries are treatable and the animal can be saved with your help. If the deer runs from the scene, you will probably never see it again. If it is injured and still on scene, you can visually inspect it for injuries. If the animal is unable to stand or is dragging its hind legs, you are most likely looking at a spinal or head injury. These deer will need to be euthanized. Deer with multiple broken legs are also beyond help. Animals showing no obvious serious injuries, or just cuts and tissue damage, may be able to be saved.

If the deer is deceased, you can take a look at the deer's belly to determine if it is a nursing female. If so, her teats will be swollen and usually a light pink color. To be sure, you can squeeze one of the teats and look for a milk discharge. If she is a "wet" doe, you must try to locate a fawn. A nursing fawn cannot survive on its own. If there is a fawn, you will usually find it near the roadway right at the place the adult deer entered the roadway. The fawn will be lying in the deep grass or brush and will be very still. They are hard to spot, but will usually be close to the road. If you find the fawn, pick it up and try to keep it calm and quiet. This is best accomplished by covering the deer and its eyes with a large towel, blanket, or jacket.

When you report the accident, you should tell the authorities that you have an orphaned animal. Ask them for a rehab contact. If you cannot get that information, contact your state fish and game department.

Domestic dogs can also cause a lot of damage to baby deer. Because the deer will not run, dogs like to grab them by a leg and drag them around the pasture. This practice usually results in a three-legged deer that can usually be saved and released. These deer need rescue.

However, most of the fawns that end up at the rehabilitation center actually don't need rescue. Well-intentioned people find the baby lying in the grass, with no mother around, and the deer doesn't seem to be able to get up. Well, unless you can bark like mom, it's not going to get up. People who like wildlife will almost always pick these animals

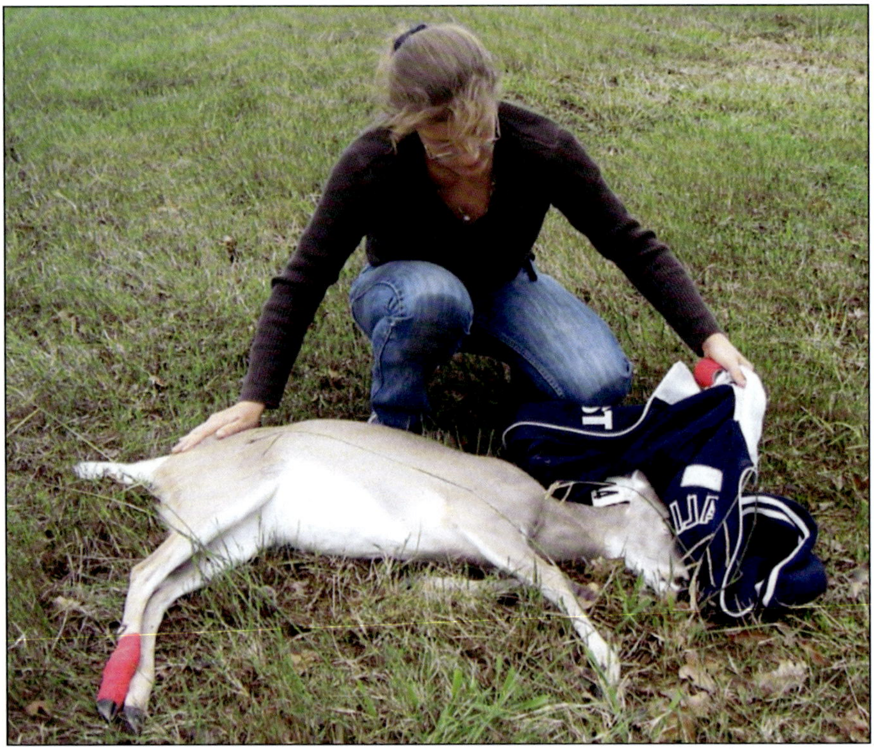

If the deer becomes excited and starts flailing, cover its head until it calms down.

up, take them home, and try to get them care. This is the most humanitarian thing to do, but it's not always in the best interest of the deer. The best thing to do when you find a fawn is to back away and leave it alone. Continue to check on it from a distance. If the fawn has been abandoned by its mother, it will start crying out. Baby deer bleat like baby sheep. The more they're stressed, the more they cry. If you have observed the baby for twelve to twenty-four hours and no mom has showed up, and the baby is crying, it probably needs rescue. Keep in mind that once a baby is picked up and moved, the possibility of ever reuniting it with mom is very unlikely.

How does one know if the deer needs rescued? First, if you walk up on a baby lying in the grass, not excited or causing a ruckus, assume the deer is fine, turn and walk away. If you come across a deer that is prancing around a pasture or road and bleating and causing a ruckus, assume the deer *may* need rescue. Based on your knowledge of deer behavior, wait and watch for as long as seems reasonable. If you find a deer with injuries, or a fawn with a dead mom nearby, rescue.

## Rehabilitation

### Intake

When receiving any animal for rehabilitation, you must first make a general assessment of its condition. You must determine if the animal is stable enough to undergo an exam and you must attend to life-threatening injuries immediately. If there is nothing that needs immediate attention, the next thing to do is to warm the animal and get it calm. Put it in a warm dark crate and let it calm down for at least an hour.

The initial exam of an incoming deer is very important. This exercise allows the rehabber to gain a complete understanding of the condition of the animal and will provide a baseline to monitor its progress as it grows.

At any time during the exam, if the deer becomes excited and starts flailing, you should stop the exam, cover the deer's head, and allow it

# *Hearts Afire Deer Rescue*

Control Number:

Date Admitted__________________

Sex ____ Aprox Age_______

Species ____________________

weight______________

temperature___________________

hydration ___________________

open wounds/broken bones

______________________________

Initial Exam/overall condition:

______________________________________________

______________________________________________

______________________________________________

| Date | Weight | | by |
|---|---|---|---|
| | | | |
| | | | |
| | | | |
| | | | |
| | | | |
| | | | |
| | | | |
| | | | |
| | | | |
| | | | |
| | | | |
| | | | |
| | | | |
| | | | |
| | | | |

Medical records form.

to calm down. Deer are very sensitive to stress and can suffer disastrous results if left unchecked.

Before starting the next phase of the intake exam, start a medical records form. This form, which will stay with the deer until it is released, will give you a written record of the deer's overall health, and all medical and treatment procedures performed on the animal throughout its stay.

Always begin the exam by gathering the pertinent general data: weight, temperature, hydration, sex, and approximate age.

## Weight

Accurate weight is extremely important. First, the dosage of all medications administered is calculated using actual, accurate animal weight data. Second, the animal's weight gain is a direct indicator of its wellness. The weight range of deer is typically between 5 and 200 pounds.

Baby deer are easy to weigh and their weight is easy to monitor. Baby deer on a milk formula should be weighed at least every other day and should show a constant weight gain at every weighing. If a gain is not realized, the deer is not progressing properly. Weight loss coupled with diarrhea is usually an indication of an incompatibility of formula, but there are several conditions that can have the same results, such as parasites, internal injuries, and diseases. Changing to a different type of milk may be required. Any time a deer's diet is changed, it will almost always get diarrhea for several days. Extreme care must be taken to avoid making a bad situation worse by adding diarrhea and further dehydration to an animal already suffering from formula problems. Close and careful daily monitoring and hydration therapy should be employed. If the issues do not start to show improvement after several days, consult your veterinarian.

Adult deer are not as easy to weigh. They are very strong, stress easily, and don't like to sit still. Rather than monitoring progress by weight, it is easier to monitor the deer by observation of behavior. Watch the deer's eating habits, its sleeping habits, its energy level, its awareness level and alertness. If the deer is not acting normal, there is probably something wrong. Look for injuries, parasites, and infections.

## Temperature

Body temperature is also an important parameter in determining the well-being of the animal. A deer's normal body temperature is 101.1°F. Temperatures above 101.1° usually indicate an infection while temperatures below 101.1° usually indicate that the deer needs to be warmed up.

If the body temperature is between 99° and 103°, it is considered within the normal range and no remediation is taken. If the temperature is below 99°, the baby deer should be warmed with heating pads and generally given a shot of Banamine (0.1cc / 10 pounds) for discomfort. Adult deer are put in a warm environment and monitored. Temperature should recover within about two hours.

If the temperature is above 103°, the deer should be treated with a dose of antibiotic. Temperature should return to normal in about twenty-four hours.

## Hydration

Body fluids are vital for the survival of all animals. Without the proper amount of fluids, the body's internal transport mechanisms will cease to function and the animal will die. When an animal suffers from injury or sickness, it is likely to also suffer from shock and dehydration.

A healthy animal will naturally maintain a balanced fluid level. Water makes up about 60 to 80 percent of body weight. It is distributed in the body as extracellular fluid (outside the body cells) and as intracellular fluid (within the body cells). It is also found in the blood plasma space. Under normal conditions, animals will naturally eliminate fluids at the rate of about 5 percent of body weight per day. These fluids are replaced daily from food and water ingested by the animal.

If an animal becomes injured or sick, the rate of fluid elimination increases, the animal becomes dehydrated, and can quickly reach critical levels. In this case, fluids must be replaced.

**Determining Hydration**

There are several factors that must be considered prior to administering fluids to an injured animal. To avoid shock, highly stressed and critical patients should be warmed and stabilized prior to hydration therapy. To determine the extent of dehydration, pinch the skin in the middle of the animal's back into the shape of a tent (called tenting) and then release the skin. If the skin returns quickly (< 1 sec.) to its original position, the hydration level is normal. The longer the skin takes to return to its original position, the more dehydrated the animal is. If the skin remains in the tent position, dehydration is at a critical level.

There are three steps required for fluid replacement:

1. **Estimate the fluid loss.** This estimate is made by observing clinical signs.

| % Loss | Clinical Signs |
| --- | --- |
| <5% | No detectable abnormalities. Skin tent <1 sec. |
| 6% | Very slight loss of elasticity. (tent return ~1-2 sec.) |
| 8% | Ten return 1-3 sec. Dry mucus membranes, dry gums. |
| 10-12% | Tent return >3 sec. Lethargic, increased heart rate, cool extremities |
| 12-15% | No tent teturn. Shock, very dry gums and eyes. |

2. **Calculate fluid replacement needs.** This is done using the following formula.

   Animal's ideal body weight* in kg x % hydration = amount of fluids (liters) needed.

   *Ideal body weight = actual body weight + 10 percent of actual body weight

For example, a 10kg raccoon, 8 percent dehydrated would have an ideal body weight of

10 kg + 1kg (10% of 10kg) = 11kg

Using the formula

11kg x 8% = 0.88 liters of fluid needed

Replacement fluids should be administered in three sessions over a twenty-four-hour period. If the hydration percentage is 10 percent or greater, you should front load the fluid delivery. To front load, give 50 percent of needed fluid in first session, then two later sessions at 25 percent each. This first administration can be given in the field at the time of rescue.

After the initial day of fluid replacement, the animal will need maintenance fluids each day until its condition improves. Maintenance fluids are given three times a day. The amount of fluids needed is calculated using the following formula:

Animal's ideal body weight* in kg x 5% = amount of fluids (liters) needed

Using the same example as above:

11kg x 5% = 0.55 liters of fluid needed

**Helpful conversions**

1kg = 2.2 pounds = 1000g
1 pound = 0.454kg
1 liter = 1000 ml
1 oz = 30 ml

3. **Determine the type of fluid to administer and the method of administration.**

There are four common methods of fluid administration: oral, subcutaneous, intravenous, and intra-osseous. The method is usually dependent on the severity of dehydration.

**Oral (PO)** should be chosen as the preferred method when possible. It is the least invasive method and is especially effective for cases where the estimated dehydration is <7 percent. Solutions given PO should contain sodium, glucose, bicarbonate, and amino acids, and do not need to be sterile. Some common choices for PO administration include Pedialyte®, Normosol®, lactated Ringer's solution (LRS), and Gatorade® (diluted 50 percent). Fluids should be administered at body temperature. PO should not be used if the patient is vomiting, or has dull senses or significant dehydration.

**Subcutaneous (SQ)** is the injection of fluids with a needle or catheter under the skin. This is the easiest method and is recommended for rescue personnel. Fluids can be administered in large volumes (do not exceed 25 ml/kg) at multiple injection sites. SQ fluids are generally absorbed within eight hours. SQ fluids should contain isotonic concentrations of electrolytes. Some of the most common SQ fluids include lactated Ringer's, normal saline 0.9%, and Normosol. A 5 percent dextrose solution can be added to LRS in a ratio of 1:3 to provide extra calories.

**Intravenous (IV)** is the administration of fluids through a catheter directly into a vein. Animals in shock or suffering from severe dehydration should be treated using this method. IV catheters can be placed in peripheral veins or directly into the jugular vein. This is a sterile process and should be administered by a veterinarian.

**Intraosseous (IO)** is the most rapid method of introducing fluids. It utilizes a spinal needle and injects fluid directly into the bone marrow, which provides a direct route to the circulatory system. This method is a sterile procedure, very invasive, highly susceptible to infection, and should only be used by a veterinarian.

## Physical Exam

After gathering the pertinent general data, a more specific exam can continue. To minimize the possibility of missing vital information, the examiner should always follow the same procedures. Start the exam at the head of the animal and work toward the rear. For best results, complete the entire exam before starting treatments. This will aid the examiner in doing a complete exam without getting sidetracked.

Starting at the head, do a comprehensive scan of the entire body looking for any external parasites, especially fleas and ticks. Run your hand against the grain of the hair looking closely at the skin. You will usually see fleas jumping as your hand moves across the hair but it is not uncommon to feel embedded ticks before you see them. If you detect parasites, treat the animal with flea and tick powder, ivermectin, or some other commercially available treatment. As a preventive measure, every animal taken in should routinely be treated for internal parasites with a commercially available wormer (e.g. Strongid® – pylantle pamoate). The worming treatment should be repeated at week four and again at week six.

The next step in the exam is looking in the mouth. The animal's gums should be clean and pink. If they are pale and gray, there is a problem. Gray gums are an indicator usually associated with disease, blood issues (anemia), or parasite activity. These animals don't eat well, refuse to stand for long periods of time, and are usually lethargic. Infectious diseases of deer can be caused by pathogens that include viruses, bacteria, parasites, and abnormal proteins known as prions. In rare instances, these pathogens are the cause of disease epidemics that result in significant mortality in a local population. These outbreaks are most common in herds with high deer density, which can increase the spread of the disease.

Also examine the inside of the nose and ears. It is not uncommon to have external parasites (including maggots) housed in these dark warm cavities. Remove parasites found in the nose and ears. The ears are a common place to find mites. Mites are best removed using Tresaderm ivermectin ear wash. Ears should be washed every day until mites are gone.

The above-mentioned full-body parasite exam will also uncover any skin wounds the deer may be suffering from. Wounds that are not bleeding severely should be cleaned and bandaged. Remove any foreign material from the wound and then clean in and around it by flushing. Use a large syringe without needle, filled with sterile water, Nolvasan® or saline solution. After cleaning, treat wound with iodine, alcohol, or hydrogen peroxide. Apply a clean, dry pad over the wound and hold in place with vet wrap. If the wound is deep and will require stitching, a moist gauze pad can be placed against the wound to keep the tissue moist.

### Suturing Wounds

If the deer presents with a wound that is too deep for routine bandage repair, suturing will probably be necessary. Living as we do in this world of vast expanses of barbed wire, knowing how to suture wounds can greatly simplify rehabilitating roaming animals.

Administering sutures requires some practice but is a useful skill to possess. To suture wounds you will need the following:

- Absorbable sutures
- Non-absorbable sutures
- Alcohol or hydrogen peroxide
- Needle holder
- Gloves

Before attempting to repair a wound, you must:

1. **Calm the animal.** To do this you can cover the animal's head with a towel, then firmly hold the animal down and wait for calming to occur, or you can administer a sedative. If you chose to use drugs, you should consult a vet.
2. **Clean and disinfect the wound:**
    - Clean with saline, alcohol, or hydrogen peroxide.
    - Use pet clippers to remove hair from wound area if possible.
    - Be sure all foreign material is cleaned out of the wound.
    - Use a local anesthesia if animal is not anesthetized. If you don't have the needed drugs, contact your vet.

*After repairing wound, administer antibiotics.* If you don't have the needed drugs, contact your vet.

There are many different stitches, many different knots, and many different techniques. When stitching an animal for rehabilitation, we tend to keep the process as simple and easy as possible. Our preference is to use a simple interrupted suture pattern and a simple square knot.

If the wound is deep into a muscle, you may need to use absorbable suture material and secure the muscle below the skin surface. Once the muscle is secure, you can stitch the skin surface. Unless you have suture training, it is probably best to leave deep wounds to the vet.

Begin by inserting the needle into the skin on one side of the wound and bring it out on the other side of the wound.

Next, place the needle holder onto the long end of the suture material (see figure 1, next page). Lift the suture material and, moving it clockwise, bring it around the needle holder forming a loop around the holder (figure 2). Take hold of the short end of the suture material and

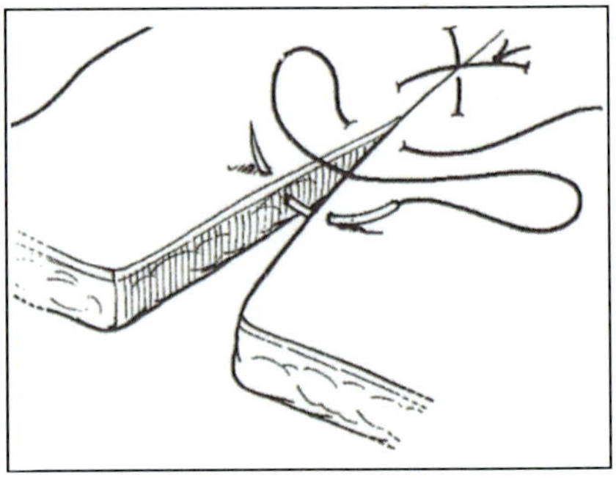

Interrupted suture pattern.

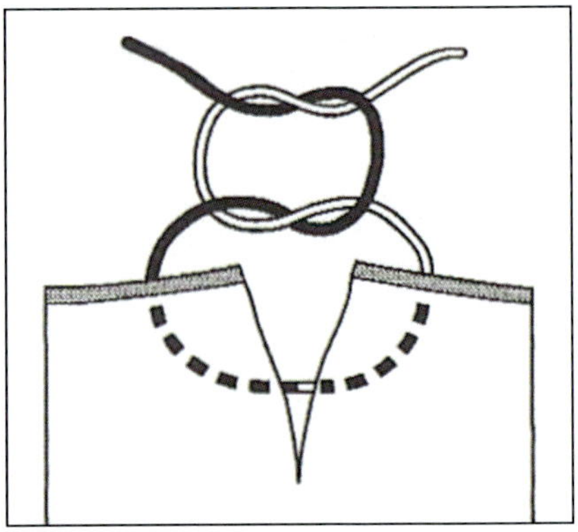

Simple square knot.

An orange is a good medium on which to practice stitching.

pull it through the loop you made around the holder (figure 3).

Pull the two ends of the suture material, forming the first half of the square knot. Place the needle holder on the long end of the suture material and repeat the wrap-and-tie process. This will give you the locking second half of the square knot securing the stitch.

Cut the material loose, move the needle over about 3/8 inch from the first stitch, and put in another stitch. Repeat this process until the wound is fully closed.

## Feeding

After the deer has settled into the rehab facility, it must be started on a suitable diet. The older the deer, the easier it is to

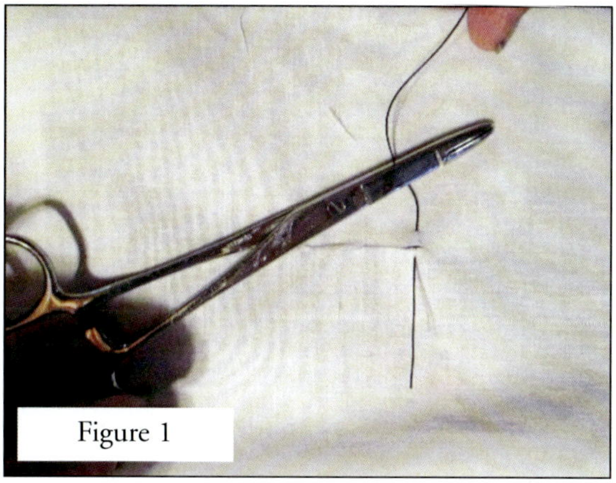
Figure 1

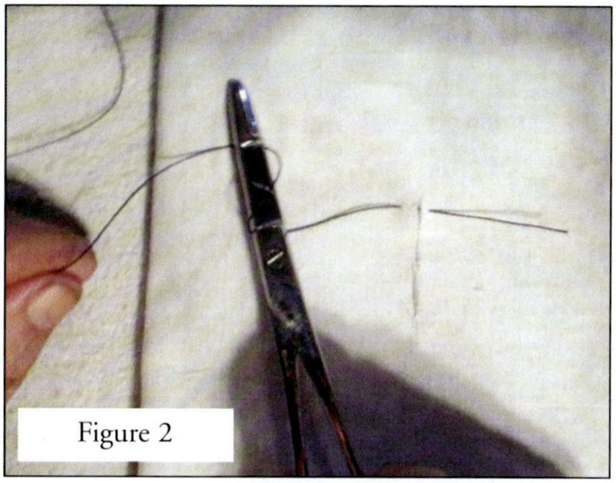
Figure 2

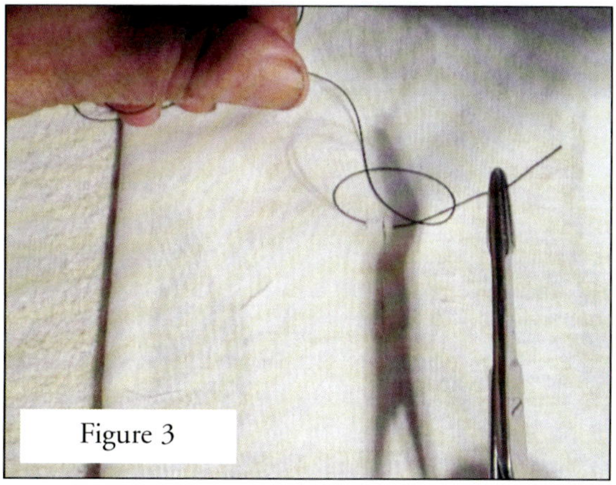
Figure 3

feed. It is not uncommon to get newborn deer into rehab. These animals usually weigh between 5 and 10 pounds and are often picked up before they have adequate time to get the needed colostrum from their mother. It is therefore the responsibility of the rehabilitator to give colostrum. A commercial colostrum substitute (Colostrx®) is available and can easily be added to the baby's formula for the first several days. If the intake examination shows slight to moderate dehydration, a pediatric electrolyte like Pedialyte® can also be added to the formula at a ratio of one quarter part Pedialyte® to mixed formula.

Selecting a formula for an infant animal must be done with care. The best formula is the natural mother's milk. This, however, is not practical because it is difficult to come by. Cow's milk is a bad choice because it is very thin (low percent of solids) and causes diarrhea and general nutrition problems. Many of the proteins and vitamins are lost when heated. Evaporated milk is concentrated cow's milk and has similar problems.

There are a variety of milk replacers available but careful selection is also important. The most common ones used in rehabilitation are KMR® (Kitten Milk Replacer), Esbilac® (dog milk replacer), Multi-milk®, and Zoologic®.

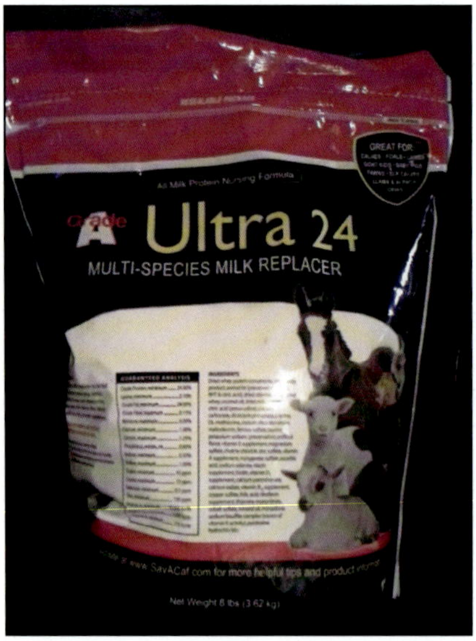


Generic Multi-milk.

Esbalac® and KMR® have been around for many years and have both worked well with wild animals. Both of these products contain extra fat, which makes them somewhat greasy. Zoologic® was developed as a replacement milk specifically for wild and exotic animals. It is very similar to the composition of KMR® except it has a lower fat

Multiple deer require a multiple feeding station.

content and is not oily. It is a popular product, widely used and nutritionally sound.

Multi-milk® is lactose- and sugar-free. It is less expensive than the others and works well. It is nutritionally sound and is our choice for rehabilitating deer.

When mixing Multi-milk®, use one part milk powder to two parts warm water and mix until smooth. Take out the amount to be fed and heat it with warm water or in the microwave until it is approximately 100°F. Do not overheat. The formula needs to be well stirred and warmed for each animal.

After opening, Multi-milk® can be stored in a freezer for up to six months beyond the expiration date. Mixed formula can be stored in a freezer in an airtight container for up to six weeks.

In the literature, there are several logarithms published that are designed to calculate the amount of formula per feeding. These calculations do not result in consistent data and therefore we only use them for ballpark reference points for mixing formula.

We have had the best success by letting the animal eat as much as it wants at each feeding on a schedule that does not promote overeating. One must always keep in mind the idiosyncrasies of the specific species. For example, opossums, like all marsupials, do not suckle. Baby rabbits suckle poorly; they, therefore, must be tubed. Raccoons have a tendency to overeat so their stomach bloating must be monitored.

Unlike some other mammals, deer do not overeat. When they have enough, they stop eating on their own. We feed our infant deer approximately 9 ounces, five times a day. We do not do middle of the

A standard human baby bottle works best for baby deer.

night feedings, but do not allow more than eight hours to pass between feedings.

When deer first come in, it is necessary to keep them contained so they can easily be caught for feeding. Once they begin coming to you for the bottle, you can expand their roaming area. When the deer get to about four weeks old, you can cut back to feeding three times a day, but offer 18 ounces per feeding. At about eight weeks, you can cut back to offering 9 ounces in an effort to wean the animal and begin to supplement feed with deer pellets and corn. They will quit taking the bottle at about eleven weeks and will be ready for release in about fourteen to eighteen weeks.

Deer, unlike many smaller mammals, do not need to be stimulated to urinate or defecate.

There are several types of bottles and nipples to use when feeding baby deer, but we have found that the regular human baby bottle works the best. The nipple hole usually needs to be enlarged, and different size holes will be required for different deer.

**Tube Feeding**

Occasionally baby animals, including deer, will refuse to eat or take a bottle. We have found that animals will sometimes begin to eat if they are offered a different type of nipple or a different temperature formula. However, if they refuse everything offered, it may be necessary to tube feed the baby. Tube feeding is the process of using a medical feeding tube to inject formula through the mouth directly into the stomach.

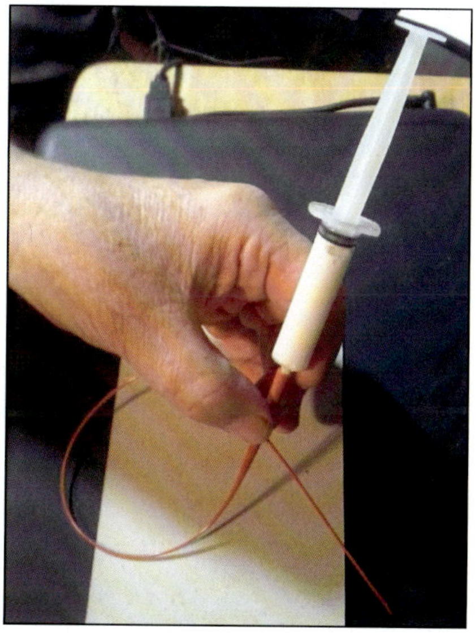

Feeding tube.

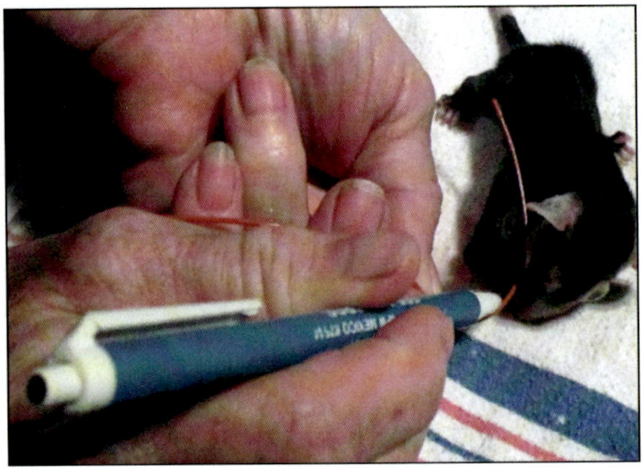

Measure and mark the tube.

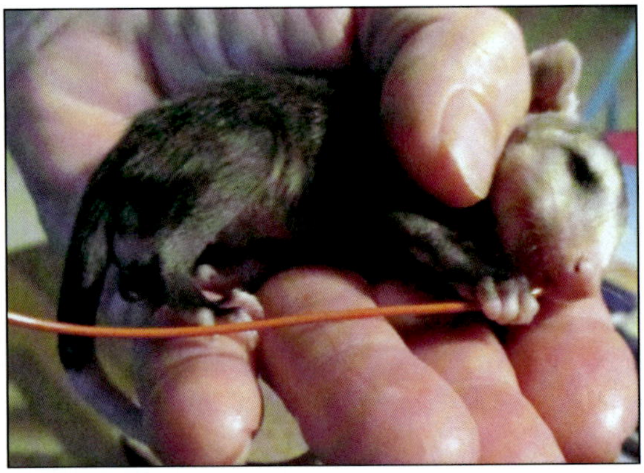

Insert tube and inject formula.

To tube feed an animal, begin by calculating the amount of food to administer. It is suggested that you use 5 percent of the animal's weight. When tubing a larger animal, like a deer, multiple injections may be necessary.

Next, measure the length of tube required to reach from the mouth to the stomach and mark the tube.

Attach a syringe containing the formula to one end of the tube and insert the other end of the tube into the animal's mouth. Slide the tube past the tongue and push it down the marked length to the stomach. You must be very careful not to inject the tube into the lungs. When inserting into the stomach, the tube should slide easily. If you feel resistance on the tube, take it out and try again. Once inserted, inject the formula into the stomach and then remove the tube.

## Weaning

Deer are ready to wean at eight to ten weeks of age. The proper method of weaning is to gradually reduce the availability of formula

Rehabbing deer are given a variety of solid food and browse.

while increasing the availability of solid food. To accommodate any changes in nutritional needs based on the deer's age and maturity, we provide a variety of solid foods (e.g., several different protein level deer pellets, both cracked corn and deer corn). We also try to keep a variety of browse available, giving the animal a wide choice of feed.

## Imprinting

One of the biggest problems facing the deer rehabber is the imprinted deer. An imprinted deer is one that is comfortable being around people. White-tailed deer imprint very quickly and most often imprint forever. They are not afraid of people and often prefer being around people. Because deer are easy to tame, extreme measures should be taken to avoid imprinting. This condition is usually caused in one of two ways: excess attention and interaction with rehabilitation staff, or people keeping deer as pets.

Once a deer enters rehabilitation, it should receive as little interaction with staff as possible. We only allow one staff member to interact

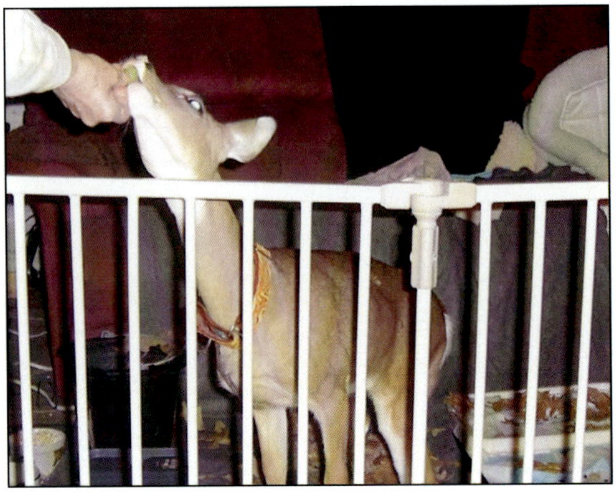

To help prevent imprinting, limit human contact to one individual.

with the deer. This person is responsible for feeding and monitoring the animal's well-being on a daily basis. No one but this single individual is allowed to be in contact with the deer. And after weaning, no one is allowed to interact with the deer except for medical maintenance.

People who pick up baby deer (which should not be picked up) and decide to keep them as pets are called "dunderheads" in the rehab field. The tame deer they produce are called "dunderdeer." People like to keep their dunderdeer in their barn or house until the deer become adults and get an attitude. These animals will eventually end up at a rehab center, either given up voluntarily by the dunderhead or confiscated by the state. Dunderdeer can seldom be reintroduced to the wild.

## Relocation

Relocating animals back into the wild is one of the things that make rehabilitation so rewarding. In the case of deer, it is also one of the most difficult parts of the process. A deer that has been handled to be wild (i.e., not imprinted and tame) and has reached an age over twenty-four weeks is difficult and dangerous to handle.

Deer are usually ready to relocate when they are fully weaned and eating only solid food and browse, and not showing signs of being dependent on their human keepers.

*Rehabilitated deer are property of the state and should not be sheltered differently than any other deer in respect to hunting. Hunting is the best management tool available to maintain a healthy herd of deer and reha-*

*bilitated deer should eventually be released back into their normal habitat. We recommend a "no hunting" release site to give deer that have been subjected to human handling a little time to acclimate to the wild.*

Deer being relocated must be captured, controlled, and transported. Unfortunately, those that are big enough to relocate don't capture, control, or transport easily. It becomes much easier if the deer is asleep. To get them asleep, we use a dart gun with a chemical restraint. Our restraint of choice for deer 50 pounds or less is Rompun®. For deer over 50 pounds, you can use a Rompun®/ketamine 50/50 mix, or a mix of telozol, Rompun®, and ketamine. Check with your veterinarian for other chemical restraint choices. Stress and high adrenaline can cancel the effectiveness of a chemical restraint, so efforts should be made to keep the deer as calm as possible until the tranquilizer takes effect.

It usually takes about twenty-five to thirty minutes for the deer to be fully restrained. Use extreme caution when approaching a sedated deer. It is not uncommon for the deer to jolt from a noise or movement. A sudden reflex from the deer can cause serious injury if prop-

It usually takes about twenty-five to thirty minutes for the deer to be fully restrained.

erly directed. If the deer is fully restrained, cover its eyes to keep it calm, and hobble its feet before trying to move it. A deer sedated by Rompun® will stay down for thirty to forty-five minutes. After transport, untie the legs and administer a Rompun® reversal. The deer should be up and walking in about five minutes.

One difficulty in larger rehab operations is deciding which animals can actually be released back into the wild. The problem is determining which animals are releasable versus those who are too imprinted to release.

When we take in a dunderdeer, we place the animal in a pasture with only wild deer and allow them no human contact. Some of these animals will herd up with the wild deer and get wild enough to release. We call these deer maybes. At release time, the maybes will get released with the herd. We have determined that about 40 percent of the deer will become wild enough to release. The other 60 percent return to the ranch or approach people looking for a handout. These deer get rescued a second time and are returned to the rehab ranch and are reclassified as dunderdeer for a second time.

At that point they are considered non-releasable and become part of the rehabilitation facility. It is important to know and understand the state's rules and policies concerning the final disposition of dunderdeer before keeping a captured deer.

## Diseases and Parasites in Deer

### Lyme Disease *(Borrelia burgdorfen)*

With deer density increasing, the spreading of infectious diseases becomes more of a concern. Increased deer populations lead to increased transmission of tick-borne diseases, which pose a threat to human health, to livestock, and to other deer. Deer are the primary host and vector for the adult black-legged tick, the lone-star tick, and the winter tick, which transmit the Lyme disease bacterium to humans. White-tailed deer also serve as intermediate hosts for many diseases that infect humans through ticks, such as Rocky Mountain spotted fever.

The white-footed mouse and the white-tailed deer carry Lyme disease, which was discovered and named a disease in the early 1980s. There are more than ten thousand cases reported each year in the U.S., giving it the distinction of being the most common tick-borne disease in the U.S. The majority of cases occur in the northeastern seaboard states, the upper Midwest, and California. Because white-tailed deer are increasing in numbers, it is probable that the geographic distribution of tick populations and, consequently, Lyme disease cases will increase accordingly.

Lyme disease is a bacterium (*Borrelia*) transmitted to humans by ticks that become infected by feeding on diseased animals, including birds, deer, rabbits, and rodents. When a tick feeds on a human, it must be attached for at least twenty-four to forty-eight hours before infection can occur. The bacteria, residing in the tick's mid-gut, migrates to the salivary gland and enters the human's blood as the tick feeds. Upon inoculation of *Borrelia* into the host's skin, an incubation period of three to thirty-two days follows before clinical disease develops.

In 90 percent of cases, initial symptoms include fever, muscle pain, lethargy, and the development of a characteristic skin lesion known as "erythema migrans." Erythema migrans is the characteristic red, annular bulls-eye lesion, which clears centrally as it expands. This lesion will spontaneously resolve, even without treatment. Untreated cases progress by being carried to many body sites: heart, muscles, bones, joints, liver, spleen, eyes, and brain. Signs usually involve the skin and musculoskeletal and nervous systems. Headaches, muscle pain, and transient joint pains often occur. The majority of cases manifest as arthritis, primarily of the large joints, especially the knee. Bouts of subtle nervous system disease such as memory loss, drowsiness, or behavioral abnormalities are characteristic. Case fatalities are rare, but patients experience a life-changing morbidity.

Procedures to avoid contact with ticks are recommended, such as wearing gloves, long pants, and long-sleeved shirts, along with conducting frequent checks of clothing and skin. When attached ticks are found, use tweezers to remove them without crushing them, and thoroughly scrub the wound.

### Rabies

Any warm-blooded mammal can carry rabies. There are, however, no reported cases of rabies infections in humans caused by deer.

### Leptospirosis *(Leptospira interrogans)*

Leptospirosis is caused by the bacterium *Leptospira interrogans* and is transmitted via urine from infected animals. Raccoons, opossums, Norway rats, mice, white-tailed deer, and striped skunks carry this disease. Striped skunks are a significant reservoir with some populations demonstrating a greater than 50 percent prevalence. Skunks can shed leptospires in their urine for up to three hundred days. Transmission occurs directly by contamination of mucus membranes or broken skin by urine. Indirectly, it can be acquired through contaminated soil and water.

The incubation period may be as short as four days or may extend for three weeks; in humans, it is usually ten days. Fever, headache, chills, vomiting, weakness, muscle pain, and conjunctivitis (inflammation of the eyelids), or a combination of these symptoms, are noted early in the disease. In the more severe infections, jaundice, kidney damage, blood disorders, and hemorrhages of the skin and mucus membranes occur.

Avoiding exposure to the urine of deer, either in handling them or coming into contact with places where they have urinated, is the primary course of protection. Protective clothes, boots, and gloves are recommended. Good personal hygiene following any potential exposure is important.

## Rocky Mountain Spotted Fever

Rocky Mountain spotted fever (tick fever) is the second most common tick-borne disease in the United States, and is caused when a human is infected by rickettsias. Rickettsias are tiny organisms between viruses and bacteria in size, which are unable to reproduce unless attached to a host; common hosts are rabbits, rodents, the Virginia opossum, and deer. The disease is transmitted from a reservoir animal to a human via ticks. The tick bites the animal, acquiring the rickettsias, then bites the human, transmitting them into the blood stream. The American dog tick in the east and the American wood tick in the west are the regional primary vectors.

After a human is bitten, there is a delay in the actual transmission of the disease-causing microorganism from the tick to the host. A reactivation process occurs, leading to a four to twenty-hour delay of infection. Human infection is characterized by a three to fourteen-day incubation period followed by nonspecific signs of the disease such as lethargy and weakness, rapidly progressing to fever, chills, headache, muscle pain, and pain in the joints. Fever is the most predictable and persistent sign. In 88 percent of the cases, generalized spotting or blotchiness of the skin starts first on the extremities, next on the palms and soles, and then rapidly spreads to the trunk. Pinpoint hemorrhages are common.

Early diagnosis and initiation of therapy, before serologic or isolation evidence, leads to a rapid uneventful recovery in most cases. In the absence of a diagnosis and specific therapy, however, a 15 to 20 percent mortality rate results. Even with effective antimicrobial therapy, a 2 percent mortality rate results in the U.S. Annually, about 50 people die from this disease; 600 to 1,200 cases are reported each year.

Avoiding contact with ticks is the primary recommendation for prevention. Wearing gloves, long pants, and long-sleeved shirts, along with conducting frequent checks of clothing and body are recommended. Remove ticks without crushing them and thoroughly scrub the wound.

## Chronic Wasting Disease

Chronic wasting disease (CWD) is a naturally occurring affliction of the brain and nervous system in deer, elk, and moose. It attacks the brain and produces small lesions that eventually result in death. CWD is similar to another disease, scrapie in sheep. No evidence exists that CWD affects humans or livestock. It was first recognized in captive mule deer in Colorado in the late 1960s, and was first documented in wild elk in Colorado in 1981. Its discovery in wild deer in south-central Wisconsin in 2002 generated heightened attention from wildlife managers, hunters, and others interested in deer. It poses a significant threat to the deer and elk of North America and, if unchecked, could dramatically alter the future management of these species. CWD does not cause an immediate widespread die-off of deer, but there may be long-term impacts to the herd if the disease is allowed to spread.

The first reported case of wild moose infected with CWD occurred in Colorado in September 2005. Because moose do not congregate like deer and elk, cases of CWD in moose are expected to remain low.

The method of CWD transmission is unknown; however, there is strong evidence to suggest that abnormally shaped proteins called prions are responsible. The agent responsible for this disease may spread directly through animal to animal contact or indirectly through soil or other surface to animal contact. It is thought that the most common mode of transmission is via saliva and feces from an infected animal. A recent study confirms that CWD prions can be shed into the environment in feces from animals showing no clinical signs of the disease and can contaminate the soil, leading to infection in other animals. It can be spread from region to region by the movement of captive deer or through the improper disposal of a harvested deer transported from a CWD-infected area.

In early stages of infection, animals show no symptoms. The incubation period can range from one to five years. In advanced stages, infected animals begin to display abnormal behavior, such as staggering or standing with very poor posture, and carrying the head and ears in a lowered position. In later stages of the disease, infected animals become emaciated. Some symptoms of CWD also may be characteristic of other diseases and conditions (e.g., bacterial brain abscesses and epizootic hemorrhagic disease, or deer that have been injured in a deer-vehicle accident).

Prior to 2008, the only method to definitively diagnose CWD was to examine the brain, tonsils, or lymph nodes in a laboratory. No live-animal test, vaccine, or treatment for CWD existed. In 2008, researchers from the USDA-APHIS and Colorado State University evaluated and validated the rectal-tissue biopsy method for detecting chronic wasting disease (CWD) in live captive and wild elk. The live rectal biopsy test appears to be nearly as accurate as a post-mortem diagnostic test.

## Brucellosis ("Undulant Fever")

Brucellosis is primarily centered in domestic agricultural species but may also be found in populations of deer, bison, elk, and caribou in the western United States. Caused by the *Brucella* bacteria, infections are usually transmitted by contamination of mucus membranes, especially by oral ingestion or through broken skin having contact with an infected animal's body fluids such as blood, urine, feces, vaginal discharges, aborted fetuses, or placentas. Aerosol transmission has also been documented.

Incubation time for brucellosis is variable, ranging from one week to several months. In humans, onset of the disease can be characterized by fever with accompanying headache, chills, profuse sweating, insomnia, sexual impotence, or joint pain.

Protective clothing should be worn when handling these animals.

## Brain Abscesses

Brain abscesses are bacterial infections in the skull and brain. In white-tailed deer, 90 percent of cases occur in bucks and are often seasonal, primarily due to the stages of antler development and fighting.

During antler drop (casting) or severe fighting with other bucks, infections can develop on the skull near the pedicle, resulting in a brain abscess. Infection symptoms may include poor coordination, circling movements, blindness, lethargy (significant lack of energy), and emaciation.

## Cutaneous Fibromas

Cutaneous fibromas are wart-like growths caused by a virus that often infects deer through an open wound or insect bite. They are most common in bucks because bucks are more likely to incur wounds while fighting and when rubbing antlers. These growths can cover large portions of the body, but they are usually small, occur in single or multiple locations, and range from a fraction of an inch to several inches in diameter.

Although sometimes grotesque in appearance, fibromas generally do no harm to deer, unless they interfere with a deer's sight or ability to eat. The virus does not infect other wild or domestic animals, or humans. Fibromas are confined to the skin and, therefore, are removed when the deer is processed for consumption. Thus, they do not affect or impact the quality of the venison.

## Infections and Injuries

Injuries may result from hunter-inflicted wounds, deer-vehicle accidents, or incidents with fences or farm equipment. Many of these injuries heal without complication, but occasionally they cause infections that create dead tissue and the presence of pus in and around the wound. Although localized infections or abscesses caused by an injury do not pose a problem to overall deer health, if an abscess is discovered, it must be trimmed out. Infections that are not abscessed must be treated with the appropriate antibiotic.

## External Deer Parasites

**Ticks:** The tick of most concern in deer is the lone-star tick *(Amblyomma americanum)*, which cause a loss of hair, anemia, and a general poor condition. Significant mortality in fawns has been reported as a direct or indirect result of heavy infestation. Other ticks that commonly infest deer include the black-legged tick and the winter tick.

Tick

**Lice:** There are two primary species that infect deer, sucking lice and chewing lice. These species are specific to deer and are seldom found on any other animals. Heavy infestations cause hair loss and irritation. Transmission is caused by direct contact with other infested deer.

*Lepotena mazamae*

***Lepotena mazamae*:** Although often referred to as deer ticks, this pest is actually a wingless fly that only infests deer. They are about an eighth of an inch long and live in the hair of the deer. They feed on blood. Infestation causes irritation, hair loss, and anemia. Heavy infestations can cause death. Transmission is from one animal to another by direct contact.

***Cephenemyia phobifer* (nasal bot):** Nasal bots are the larval stage of flies. Deer become infected when the adult fly lays its eggs in the nasal passages of the deer. They attach themselves to the nasal passage and remain there until they pupate. After about a month of pupation, adult flies emerge from the nose and fall to the ground. A deer can har-

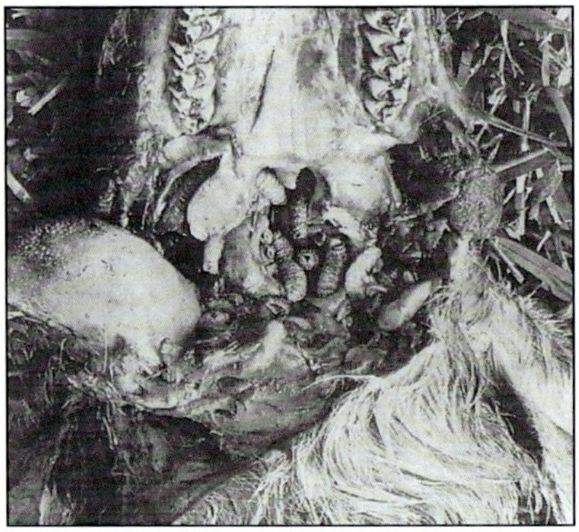

Cephenemyia phobifer

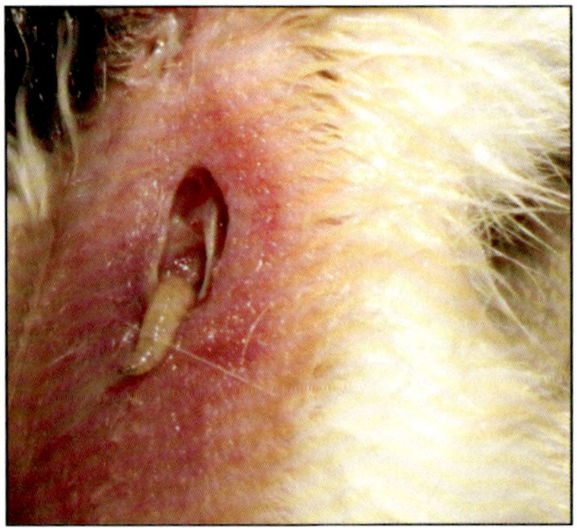

Myiasis

bor a huge number of flies, but they appear to cause little damage beyond irritation. These parasites have also been found in the lungs, stomach, and esophagus.

**Maggots:** Maggot is the generic term for any species of fly larvae. As with fleas and ticks, they can be a threat to household pets and wild animals. Flies reproduce rapidly in the summer months and maggots can come in large numbers, creating a maggot infestation and a high risk of myiasis. Myiasis is the parasitic infestation of the body of a live mammal by fly larvae (maggots) that grow inside the host while feeding on its tissue. Humans are not immune to the feeding habits of maggots and can also contract myiasis. When maggots turn into adult flies and start the life cycle over, numbers will grow exponentially if unchecked. This can result in a spread of the myiasis and increasing lesions, which in time can cause death. If maggots or other parasitic worms are detected during an exam, they need to be removed. This is usually accomplished by manually removing them one at a time with tweezers or forceps. If chemical removal is preferred, you can apply Capstar®.

## Internal Deer Parasites

Deer are also susceptive to a variety of internal parasites that can cause a whole host of problems. Issues associated with internal bugs are hard to spot and identify during an initial exam. We have found that the best way to prevent problems with internal parasites is to proactively treat all incoming deer for parasite infection as a routine intake protocol.

**Internal Parasites:**

- Cause irritation
- Cause diarrhea
- Transmit diseases
- Ingest blood and lymph, causing anemia
- Secrete toxins
- Cause internal blockages
- Cause tissue damage
- Produce traumatic lesions
- Cause psychosomatic disease (make animals restless)
- Disrupt metabolic function
- Reduce weight gain and feed utilization
- Cause zoonotic infections

Using Strongid® (pylantle pamoate), every deer is treated (wormed) as part of its initial examination and then again in week four and week six. If the routine worming doesn't eliminate the infection issues, a fecal float procedure is performed in an attempt to obtain more specific information. Fecal floatation concentrates eggs and oocysts present in the feces of an animal into a drop of solution for easy identification.

Many rehabilitation facilities avoid doing fecal floats because a high-dollar microscope is required. Over the years, we have figured out that many of our cooperating vets are willing and often eager to help with disease analysis using their equipment. If a rehabber does a fecal float and only needs a look through the scope to complete the process, he may find himself encouraged to do the scope work at the vet's office.

**Fecal Float Test**

To do a fecal float test, begin by gathering the following materials:

- Small container to soak fecal matter. A discarded pill bottle works well.
- Fecal solvent (see below).
- Gauze pad
- Stir rod
- Float tube – a small test tube works well
- Microscope slide cover
- Microscope slide

You can use commercial fecal solvent (Fecasol®) or you can make your own solvent by mixing 28g granulated sugar (sucrose) into 1 ounce of tap water. This will produce a solution with a specific gravity of 1.27, suitable to dissolve fecal material and float eggs and oocysts.

Begin by placing a fecal sample, about the size of a dime, into your soak container. Add solvent until fecal matter is fully covered and mix well with stir rod.

Allow the fecal material to soak in the solvent for at least twenty minutes. This gives the target eggs and oocysts time to separate from the raw fecal material and float freely in the solution.

Place your gauze over the top of the soak container, and pour the liquid through the gauze (filtering out all solid material) into the float tube. Fill the float tube to the top with filtered solvent and allow the liquid to form a raised cap (convex meniscus) of liquid on the top of the tube.

To collect the target material, place the slide cover onto the top of the float tube. Be sure that the liquid covers the underside of the slide cover.

Allow the float tube and slide cover to sit for at least twenty minutes. This allows the target material to float to the top of the float tube and collect on the slide cover. After twenty minutes, remove the slide cover and place it on a microscope slide. The slide is now ready to be examined under a microscope.

1. Put a fecal sample about the size of a dime into your soak container.

2. Place your gauze over the top of the soak container.

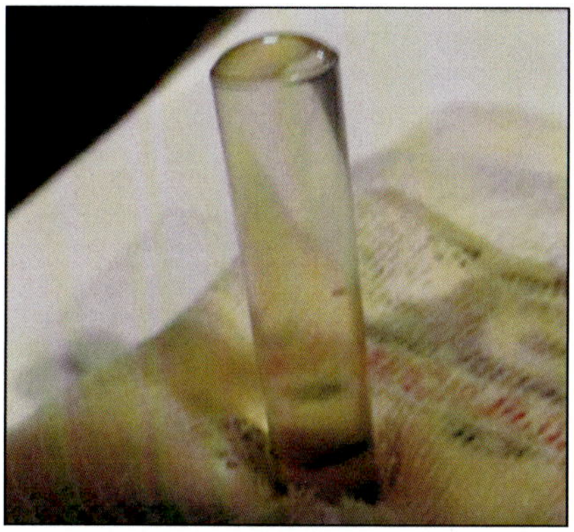

3. Fill the float tube to the top and allow the liquid to form a raised bubble of liquid on the top lip of the tube.

4. Note placement of slide cover. Leave in place for twenty minutes.

5. Remove the slide cover and place it on a microscope slide.

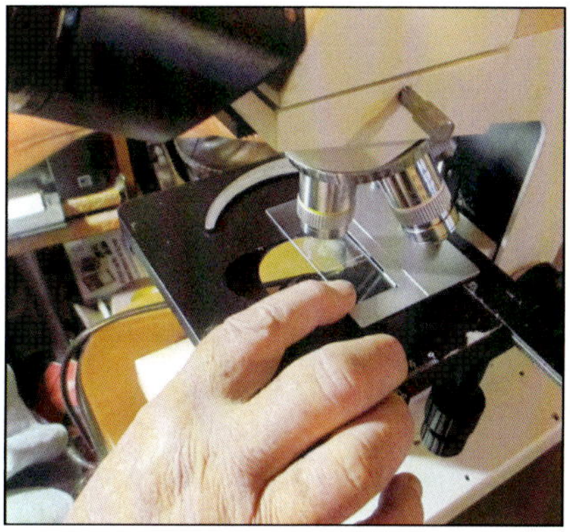

6. Examine under a microscope.

**Skunks at a Glance**

| | |
|---|---|
| Gestation Period | 60 to 65 days |
| Weight at Birth | 20 to 40 grams |
| Formula | KMR® |
| Frequency of feeding babies | 5x/day |
| Weaned | 50 days |
| Reproduction | Once, in spring |
| Litter size | 4 to 8 |
| Adult weight | 12 to 16 pounds |
| Hibernation | No |
| Natural foods | Insects, worms, fruits, dog food, garbage, birds, bird eggs |
| Normal temperature | 97°F |

Chapter Two

# Skunks

## Introduction

Skunks are probably the most hated and misunderstood animals, while at the same time, they are among the kindest, gentlest creatures in the animal world. Unless they are provoked into spraying their noxious spray, they can live under your house and go unnoticed for years. These docile, slow-moving animals dispose of insects and small rodents, and if they didn't spray, would soon become the most loved animal on the farm. They seldom get excited, hardly ever fight with other animals, and are quite intent on minding their own business. Their high-contrast black and white colors seem to advertise the fact that they are there and are not afraid of anyone. When threatened, they engage their powerful defense mechanism and discharge a scent that will stop almost any attacker. This spray is so potent that it can be detected for more than one-half mile.

Some people think the skunk's spray comes from its urine. This is not true. It actually is emitted from the animal's anal glands through tube-like ducts. Adult skunks carry about a tablespoon of this noxious spray, a sulfur-alcohol solution known as butylmercaptan. They can control the discharge rate, allowing them to spray up to 15 feet with high precision, and up to five times in a very short period. Baby skunks

Skunks warn before they spray. If you get this view, it's usually too late.

discharge their entire supply of chemical in one shot.

Skunks almost always give warning before they spray. They stomp their front feet, spin in circles, and raise their tail. If the threat does not disappear, the skunk will turn its tail toward the victim and spray. After the skunk releases its spray and the threat goes away, it will continue on as if nothing happened. Skunks spray only when threatened and, in areas with no threat, can live with their human hosts for years totally undetected.

Skunks have very strong forefeet and long nails, making them excellent diggers. Much of the skunk's diet is found by digging. They will spend considerable time digging up earthworms in nicely planted lawns. Like other members of the Mustelidae family, skunks have small feet with five toes on each foot. The tracks are often confused with cat tracks. Cat tracks are the same size and shape but only have four toes and don't show claw marks. Skunk tracks almost always display the long claws.

Skunks have a territorial range of only thirty to forty acres. In the wild, they live in shallow burrows, in caves, or under logs. In urban and suburban settings, the skunk has found suitable homes in and under outbuildings, under decks, in garages, and in woodpiles. They like dry, dark, and defensible areas, which are easily found in or around almost any home. Skunks are nocturnal and begin feeding at sunset.

Mating takes place in February through March. The gestation period varies by species, and the female gives birth to between four and eight young. The babies are born with their eyes closed and are completely helpless. They nurse for about two months. The mother skunk is fiercely protective of her young.

Skunks do not hibernate, but during the cold winter months, they enter into a period of greatly decreased activity. They are not highly social animals but will gather in communal winter dens. In one instance, more than five hundred skunks were found living under a barn in Nebraska.

Front- and hind-foot tracks of a striped skunk.

There are many theories about when skunks can and cannot spray. Many people have been told and believe that a skunk in a trap cannot spray because it cannot raise its tail. We can personally assure the reader that this is not true. Over the years, we have captured full-grown striped skunks in small squirrel traps. These poor creatures couldn't even take a deep breath, much less raise their tail. But when a threat is detected, the tail moves to the side and a shot is fired. Even in these cramped quarters, their aim is very good.

Another theory that we suggest you dismiss is the idea that a skunk won't spray if you hold its tail down. True, it won't be able to spray out to its normal effective range, but it sure can release enough spray onto its tail to ruin the day for even the best tail-holder. Others will tell you they won't spray if their hind feet are off the ground. If you believe this, good luck.

It has been our experience that when a skunk feels the need to spray, it's going to spray.

The only real predators of the skunk are raptors, especially the great horned owl, and humans. Skunks are slow movers and easy to spot. Although their spray is enough to keep other predators away, most raptors do not have a sense of smell.

There are three genera of skunks in the United States: the hog-nosed skunk *(Conepatus euconotus)*, the spotted skunk *(Spilogale putorius)*, and the most common, the striped skunk, which has two species, the common skunk *(Mephitis mephitis)* and the hooded skunk *(Mephitis mecroura)*. Spotted skunks are the only ones able to climb trees.

Hog-nosed skunk – *Conepatus euconotus*

Spotted skunk – *Spilogale putorius*

Striped skunk – *Mephitis mephitis*

Hooded skunk – *Mephitis mecroura*

# Rehabilitation

## Intake

The protocol used for intake of skunks is basically the same as that for deer: make a general assessment, warm the animal, perform the initial exam, start a medical record, and obtain vitals. Always start the exam at the head, working toward the tail, and always complete the entire exam before administering treatment.

As skunks are slow-moving animals, they are susceptible to being hit by cars. This often results in litters of baby skunks left without a mother. It would be difficult to find a baby animal more adorable than a tiny skunk. Because they are so cute and cuddly, rescuers of these litters often want to keep and raise them. This is a bad idea.

When first born, baby skunks cannot spray. At five to six weeks, however, they begin to produce a musky odor and will be able to spray shortly thereafter. Baby skunks, unlike adults, cannot regulate the amount of spray they emit. This means that the little ones can be just as potent as the big ones.

At birth, skunks weigh from 20 to 30 grams and have a normal body temperature of 97.2°F. They are born with their eyes closed and

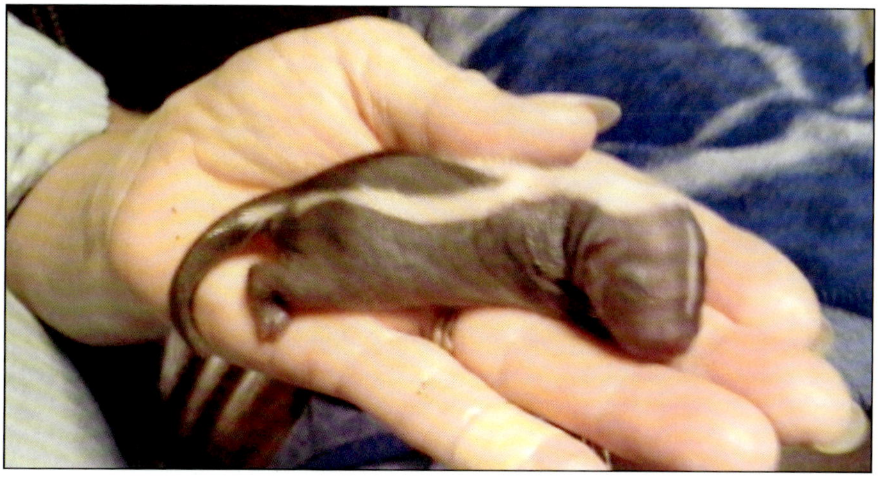

Intake skunk – 25 grams

are totally helpless. The mother stays with them except when she leaves the nest to feed.

Skunks scheduled for release back into the wild should be vaccinated against feline panleukopenia and canine distemper. For feline panleukopenia we recommend Fel-O-Vax LVKIIIA®, and for canine distemper we suggest Vanguard 5/L4®. Although illegal in most states, skunks do make reasonable (albeit destructive) family pets. Pet skunks should be vaccinated the same as a pet cat.

## Weight

Baby skunks are tiny and are weighed in grams rather than pounds. A typical baby will weigh under 100 grams. The measure for all animals' health profile is obtained by monitoring weight gain. However, with an animal that can eat 5 percent of its body weight at a feeding, a change of a few grams can look significant when it's really not. Therefore, for lightweight animals like baby skunks, the weight should be taken and monitored weekly rather than daily.

Watch the skunk's eating habits, its sleeping habits, its energy level, its awareness level, and its alertness. If the skunk is not acting normal

The weight of baby skunks is measured in grams.

and is losing weight, there is probably something wrong. Look for diarrhea, injuries, formula incompatibilities, parasites, and infections.

## Temperature

The normal body temperature of a skunk is 97.2°F. Because of their small size, it is difficult to get a rectal body temperature without injuring the animal. We, therefore, do not recommend monitoring body temp. Instead, watch the animal for external signs of infection: mucus discharge from the eyes and nose, lethargic behavior, and hot tummy. If it appears that the animal has an infection, treat it with Bactrum. This is a milder antibiotic that it not too harsh for the small animal. Bactrum should be administered PO.

## Hydration

As with any animal, without the proper amount of fluids, the body's internal transport mechanisms will cease to function and the animal will die. Being of such small stature, skunks can usually be rehydrated orally. Mix an electrolyte solution at a ratio of 1:3 electrolyte to formula. The hydration level in skunks can be determined using the same method as discussed in Chapter One – Deer.

## Feeding

Skunks are typically easy to care for and feed. Baby skunks usually come in, eyes closed, at around 20 to 40 grams.

Skunks develop better on a higher fat content formula so we use KMR® (Kitten Milk Replacer) rather than Multi-milk®. Like all animals, the newborns need colostrum and for the first few days their formula can be supplemented with Colostrx®. Their hydration must also be maintained, which can, because of their small size, usually be accomplished orally with electrolytes.

Mother skunks spend their nights out foraging, which means the babies usually eat during the day. This makes rehabbing them much more convenient; we do not provide night feedings but don't exceed

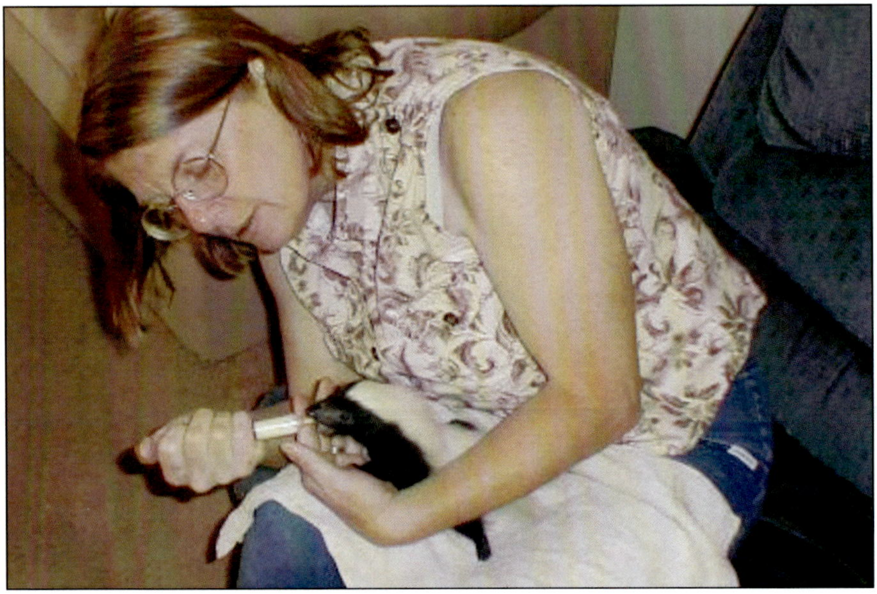

Feeding a hog-nosed skunk

more than eight hours between feedings. We feed baby skunks five times a day and usually offer 1cc to 2cc per feeding. When they are about six weeks old, we switch to a three feeding per day schedule and offer as much as they want to eat.

Baby skunks can overeat, so they should not be offered more than 5 to 7 percent of their body weight per feeding. The newborns should be fed at a minimum of every two hours until their initial weight has at least doubled. They can then be switched to a four-hour schedule. Their weight should be checked weekly to ensure they are developing properly. If a baby loses weight two weeks in a row, reevaluate your choice of formula. If it gets diarrhea, cut back on its feedings, and if this condition continues, seek assistance.

As long as eyes are closed, the baby must be stimulated to urinate and defecate. Baby skunks open their eyes at twenty-one days. The mother skunk stimulates by licking the anus. The rehabber uses a warm damp cloth, rubbing gently.

Almost everyone is concerned about being sprayed when handling skunks. This isn't a problem for newborns because skunks can't spray until about six weeks of age. After six weeks they have accepted their caregiver as family and seldom feel the need to spray.

At about seven weeks, the babies should have their diet supplemented with solid foods. Vegetables, eggs, dog food, and chicken are good choices. The adult diet should consist of at least 60 percent vegetables and no more than 5 percent fruit. Keep protein intake to a minimum. You should also avoid red meat, pork, cat food, high-protein dog food, chocolate, fried foods, high-fat-content foods, and sunflower seeds.

## Weaning

At six weeks, when skunks become "armed," it is a good idea to begin weaning them. Skunks should be fully weaned at about eight weeks.

To begin the weaning process, offer wet cat or dog food. Reduce the number of bottle feedings by one every two days. After a week, offer a dry version of the same cat or dog food; keep a bowl of dry food available 24/7. You can also give them an egg and any bugs you can catch.

A skunk can be released back into the wild when it is eating all hard natural food and is about eighteen weeks. Its normal diet consists of insects, rodents, berries, fruits, dog food, garbage, birds, bird eggs, and worms.

## Imprinting

Skunks will easily imprint and caution must be taken not to overhandle these creatures. Although the first rule of rehabilitation is that wild animals are not pets, skunks thrive around humans and are gentle and kind. In fact, they are so social, so cute, and so affectionate, it is tempting to keep them as pets. They actually have the best traits of

Domestic skunks: champagne and smokey colored

both cats and dogs: they come when they are called, they don't bark, they will sit in your lap, they kill mice, and they will use a litter box.

I'm just sayin'!

## Relocation

Before releasing the skunks, it is important to see if they are capable of hunting and finding food on their own. Place a cake pan full of sand into their habitat and bury some live mealworms in the sand. Put the skunks in the cage and watch to see if they can detect, uncover, and eat the worms. If they find their prey, they are ready for release. If they don't find the worms, start feeding the skunks mealworms on a daily basis and retest in a week.

Relocating skunks can be a tricky business. Although one of the gentlest creatures in the animal world, many people don't care for them and certainly do not want them around their residence. Skunks are non-territorial, and will do best if released away from people but close to good cover and a source of water. Any habitat that has available water will usually have an ample supply of food. Skunks like to feed on bugs and do really well in a wet, bug-infested environment.

When skunks are relocated to a new area, they usually start ambling along, looking for something to eat. If they find enough, they will be content to stick around. They will feed throughout the night and then find space under a log or rock and go to sleep. Our experience indicates that relocated skunks do not attempt to return to their last home but go wherever there's food.

## Diseases in Skunks

### Rabies

Anytime someone mentions rabies, everyone automatically thinks skunks. Myth has it that skunks are natural carriers of rabies, skunks are born with rabies and, if a skunk is out during daylight, they have rabies. None of this is true. There is a high occurrence of rabies in the species, but the reason is that skunks are very social animals and share habitat with other groups of skunks. Close social living conditions allow an easy spread of any type of disease. Skunks infected with rabies will perish after about fifteen days.

There are seven distinct variants or strains of rabies that affect land mammals as well as an unknown number that affect bats. The various strains appear dominant in different geographic regions. Since 1960, rabies in the United States has been more frequently reported in wild than in domestic animals. Wildlife now accounts for more than 90 percent of all rabies cases.

Raccoons, skunks, foxes, coyotes, and bats account for the majority of cases in the United States, although any warm-blooded mammal can carry rabies. Coyote rabies has reached epizootic (attacks many animals in a region at the same time) proportions in southern Texas. Bats comprise the third largest rabies reservoir after skunks and raccoons. It is reported, however, that less than 1 percent of bat population carries the disease.

Human rabies continues to be reported in small numbers in the U.S.: twenty-four cases were reported from 1980 to 1994. Fourteen individuals were diagnosed with strains known from animal reservoirs, and ten were traced to strains associated with bats.

Most cases of rabies are the result of a bite from an infected animal. A non-bite exposure can also occur when saliva or brain tissue from an infected animal enters open skin or mucous membranes (eyes, nose, or mouth).

Humans are relatively resistant to rabies. Reports indicate only 15 percent of humans bitten by a known rabid animal become infected with rabies. Reliable incubation periods range from fewer than ten days to more than six years. After initiation of clinical signs, the virus is almost always fatal.

Early signs are characterized by apprehension, headache, a low-grade fever accompanied by vague sensory changes such as discomfort and irritation or pain in the area of the bite, and swelling of the lymph nodes. Visual and auditory sensitivities may occur, causing disorientation, agitation, hallucination, and (rarely) aggression.

Difficulty swallowing due to muscle spasms and hyper-salivation leads to hydrophobia (foaming at the mouth) in approximately 50 percent of the cases. Partial paralysis and, eventually, complete paralysis ensues. Death usually results from respiratory failure one week after onset of the disease.

To help prevent rabies exposure, wear heavy gloves when handling skunks and watch for symptoms of the disease: unstable standing and walking, discharge from nose and eyes, walking in circles, and confusion.

### Bubonic Plague *(Yersinia Pestis)*

Bubonic plague is caused by a bacterium, *Yersinia pestis*, and is primarily a flea-transmitted disease that can also be acquired through direct contact with infected animals and their tissues, or by inhalation.

Plague is one of the most dangerous zoonotic diseases. There are three forms found in humans: bubonic, septicemic, and pneumonic, all caused by the same bacterium. Plague has over 200 known carriers.

Plague cases are very rarely reported in most parts of the United States. Ninety percent of the reported cases are found in New Mexico, Arizona, California, and Colorado. When rodent numbers are great and are accompanied by dense flea populations, periodic epizootics occur. These result in high mortality to the carriers, which then increases the possibility of exposure to domestic pets and humans when the fleas look for alternate hosts.

Rodent die-offs may signal the start of a period of special concern when increased precautions need to be taken. Animals that are infected by the disease will become lethargic and inactive. They can easily be approached and will usually die shortly after the disease takes hold.

After a two- to six-day incubation period, an infection emanates from the site of the flea bite. Characteristic symptoms include fever, headache, chills, muscle pain, weakness, fatigue, and upset stomach. In bubonic plague, lymph nodes become enlarged and inflamed, forming "buboes," especially in the region of first exposure. Septicemic plague is a secondary stage bubonic plague infecting the bloodstream. Those infected with septicemic plague do not present with fever or buboes. In pneumonic plague, the bacteria settle in the lungs; this form of plague can be transmitted between humans. Case fatality rates reach 50 to 60 percent in untreated cases of bubonic plague and nearly 100 percent in pneumonic cases. Death usually occurs within days.

The best prevention is to treat all incoming animals with flea and tick treatments.

### Leptospirosis *(Leptospira interrogans)*

Leptospirosis is caused by a bacterium, *Leptospira interrogans,* that is transmitted via direct contamination of mucus membranes or broken skin by urine from infected animals. Indirectly, it can be acquired through contaminated soil and water. Raccoons, opossums, Norway rats, mice, white-tailed deer, and striped skunks carry this disease. Striped skunks are a significant reservoir with some populations demonstrating a greater than 50 percent prevalence. Skunks can shed leptospires in their urine for up to three hundred days.

The incubation period may be as short as four days or may extend for three weeks; in humans it is usually ten days. Fever, headache, chills, vomiting, weakness, muscle pain, and conjunctivitis (inflammation of the eyelids), or a combination of these symptoms are noted early in the disease. In the more severe infections, jaundice, kidney damage, blood disorders, and hemorrhages of the skin and mucus membranes occur.

Avoiding exposure to the urine of skunks, either in handling them or coming into contact with places where they have urinated, is the primary course of protection. Protective clothes, boots, and gloves are recommended. Good personal hygiene following any potential exposure is important.

## Coexisting with Skunks

Like all nuisance wildlife, skunks visit humans for food, water, or shelter. Remove these attractants and the skunks will leave. Pick up outdoor pet food at night, seal around outbuildings and patios, clean up brush piles, and pick up fallen fruit. Doing these things takes time and money, and the skunks are not going to help. Coexistence with wildlife takes considerable effort, but it is certainly possible and worthwhile.

Skunks are one of the easiest and at the same time the most difficult animals to coexist with. If the animal living under a shed never feels threatened and therefore never sprays, the shed owner can be totally oblivious to its presence. If, on the other hand, the skunk feels threatened and sprays, the shed owner will want it gone right now.

Skunks eat lots of insects and small rodents and, when not causing a stink, are often referred to as the farmer's best friend. They are also very clean animals.

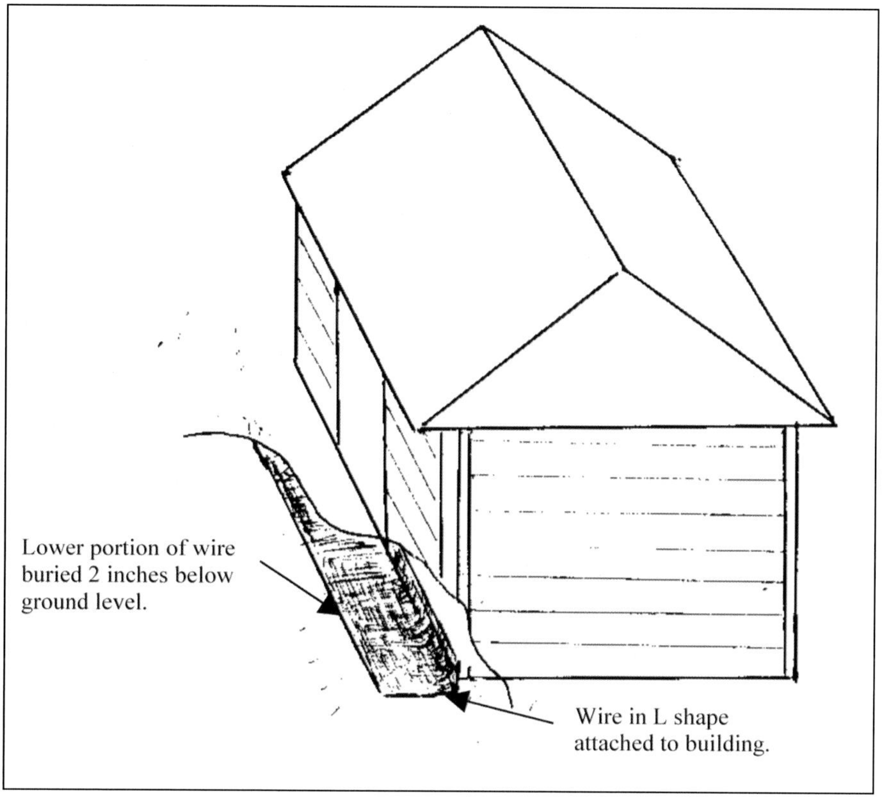


The easiest way to coexist with a skunk and take advantage of its good points is to remove anything it might perceive as a threat. Pets, especially dogs, always seem to excite skunks. To prevent dogs threatening the skunk, fence off the area around its den so the dogs can't get close. If you want the skunk to den somewhere else, remove from your property what it wants: food, water, or shelter. Skunks are not nearly as tenacious as many other animals and will generally respond to barriers installed by humans. A chain-link fence around the "no skunk zone" will usually work. Skunks (except spotted skunks) will not climb a fence. If the skunk digs its way in, attach a twelve to eighteen inch wide piece of wire screen to the fence or building you are trying to protect, bend it into an L shape, and bury the lower portion under ground.

Coexisting with skunks is the same as coexisting with any wild nuisance animal. You must keep in mind that these creatures are trying to survive in habitat we took away from them and that all concessions must be yours.

### If You Get Sprayed

Everyone seems to have a remedy for getting skunk spray off, especially off the family dog. Everything from vinegar washes to tomato juice baths has been used. Some of these will partially work, but let's face it — the stuff is hard to get off.

There are several remedies that will deodorize skunk spray.

Ozone and ion generators are commercially available machines that generate ozone and negatively charged ions. The ozone oxidizes the spray chemicals and neutralizes them. The ions react with the positive particles in the skunk spray and neutralize them. These machines are expensive but work well.

In addition, these mixtures are very effective at removing the odor:

- Mix one quart of 3 percent hydrogen peroxide with one-half cup of baking soda and one tablespoon of Dawn® dish soap. Apply this mixture to affected area and let stand for ten to fifteen minutes. Wash with warm soapy water followed by a rinse with warm clean water. Repeat if necessary. This mixture may cause some discoloration of your animal's fur. Do not store leftover mix in a closed container because the chemical reaction may cause excessive pressure and bursting of the container.
- Mix one bottle of women's medicated douche in one gallon of water. Apply this mixture to affected area and let stand for ten to fifteen minutes. Wash with warm soapy water followed by a rinse with warm clean water. Repeat if necessary.
- Tomato juice is a remedy that is well known and been used for years. Soaking in tomato juice will help, but the chemicals in

the juice that react with the skunk spray are in very small concentrations. To achieve the desired result, a very large volume of juice is required. The other methods listed above are much better.

### Raccoons at a Glance

| | |
|---|---|
| Gestation Period | 62 days |
| Weight at Birth | 100 to 200 grams |
| Formula | KMR® |
| Frequency of feeding babies | 5x/day |
| Weaned | 6 weeks |
| Reproduction | Once per year |
| Litter size | Up to 12 |
| Adult weight | 15 to 25 pounds |
| Hibernation | Semi-hibernation |
| Natural foods | Insects, worms, fruits, dog food, garbage, birds, bird eggs, small rodents |
| Normal temperature | 99.0° to 102.5°F |

Chapter Three

# Raccoons

## Introduction

When it comes to pesky wildlife, the raccoon is clearly the king. Raccoons are curious and tenacious carnivores that can be found in almost every neighborhood. They are hard to control and are known to go wherever they want, whenever they want.

Knowing the "raccoon rule" can help you understand the raccoon's behavior:

**The Raccoon Rule**

If he can see it, it's his.
If he can smell it, it's his.
If he can hear it, it's his.
If he can touch it, it's his.
If he can't touch it, it's his.
If he wants it, it's his.
and
If it's yours, it's his.

Raccoons are probably the most common backyard pests in the United States. They are found in every state and throughout most of

Canada and Central and South America. They are adaptable animals that thrive around humans. Raccoons are natural hunters on water as well as land and will eat almost anything. They prefer mature woodlands and flourish along streams, but recent studies indicate that raccoons can survive quite well in more arid climates.

In most neighborhoods, the animal's main diet consists of dog food, garbage, and pond fish. The raccoon eats at night and is known for washing its food prior to eating. There are several theories about this behavior, but published studies indicate that when raccoons are feeding around water, they use their feet to locate and identify food. Their sensitivity to touch is much greater when the feet are wet. Thus, when feeding where water is present, they submerge their food to feel it before ingestion. If no water is present, they just eat it.

Raccoons are strong animals and can be vicious if cornered. They almost always come out on top when confronted by a dog.

Raccoons do not hibernate like their cousin the bear. They do, however, go into what is called semi-hibernation during the winter months. A raccoon's metabolic rate drops, which allows it to go for several days at a time without food and water. To prepare for this, the raccoon builds a fat reserve during the fall months by going on a feeding frenzy, focusing on the many fruits that ripen during the fall season.

Raccoons rely on nature to provide the proper caloric intake for the time of year. Although many people find it tempting to feed backyard raccoons, this practice can greatly upset the animal's caloric balance and cause severe harm. Feeding raccoons the wrong food at the wrong time of year can cause the females to ovulate more than once a year and become pregnant at the wrong time of year. This phenomenon usually results in the death of the mother and the litter.

Raccoons reproduce once a year with a litter size of six to eight pups, which can be continually handled and loved by humans but will revert back to their wild instincts at about 120 days.

Many who find a baby raccoon make the decision to keep the animal as a pet because, at a young age, the raccoon readily accepts human parents and becomes loving and playful. When the baby reach-

When a raccoon feels threatened, it lowers its head, humps its back, and lets out a threatening growl.

es about eight to ten months of age, however, it reverts back to the instincts of a wild animal. At this age, the animal can become dangerous and should be trained to forage, then released.

Raccoons have sharp teeth, like a cat. Bites are usually deep and can be painful. When a raccoon bites, it often refuses to release its grip. They have very strong jaws that can cause serious damage. If they get hold of a hand or finger, they can easily crush bones. They are also tenacious animals and never give up their fight to get free.

When held down, a raccoon can generate a variety of blood-curdling sounds, from barking to growling to loud screams. Even in extreme distress, the raccoon continues to take advantage of opportunities to bite and scratch. It can also strike out with its feet, which can cause a painful injury.

The best way to confine a raccoon while trying to rescue it is to cover its head and eyes with a heavy towel and hold the scruff of the neck while pushing the head down to the ground with one hand and pushing the body down using the other hand. To pick the animal up, keep hold of the back of the neck and then grab the scruff on the back in front of the tail. If you can't get a good grip on the back, use the tail. To be successful, you must be firm and aggressive. The longer you hold the animal, the greater the chance it is going to get free or bite you.

Getting the animal into a carrier can also be a difficult task, because it will grab onto everything within reach to prevent its confinement. Again, to be successful, you must be firm and aggressive. If you let the raccoon convince you that it is being hurt and you back off, *you* will get hurt.

Raccoons can carry zoonotic diseases (diseases passed from animals to humans), are unpredictable, and can cause serious bite injuries. In most states, there is an abundance of wildlife rehabilitation facilities that have trained staff to safely work with them. Homeowners who find baby raccoons should keep the babies warm and secure and immediately contact a rehab facility. It is best not to keep the babies.

*Raccoons do not make good pets.*

## Rehabilitation

Raccoons frequently get into situations from which they require rescue and, ultimately, rehabilitation. They often seek the warmth and security of a household chimney to nest and give birth. The mother and babies must be removed from the chimney because the fireplace contains toxic soot and creosote, caustic to the newborn animals, and which can easily cause skin burns and blindness. Often, mother raccoons are killed by cars or people, leaving nests of abandoned newborns. The babies need to be rescued, rehabilitated, and relocated.

It's important to remember that these animals can be vicious and aggressive when cornered, can move quickly when defending themselves, and can cause serious injury to the rescuer. The main threat posed by raccoons comes from their teeth and their feet, especially the hind feet. When attacked by another animal, raccoons often lie on their backs, making themselves look vulnerable. When the attacking animal attacks the apparently submissive raccoon, the raccoon pulls

A group of babies rescued from a fireplace, awaiting the day of release back into the wild.

the aggressor in with its front feet and tears at the animal's underside with its powerful hind feet. It usually takes only a couple of blows until the attacker is killed. Around water, the raccoon tempts its attacker into the water by appearing to be in distress. When its attacker enters the water, the raccoon grabs it and forces it under water until it drowns. There are few predators that can take on a raccoon and win.

Unlike many other animals, raccoons don't show a lot of fear of humans and therefore adult raccoons are dangerous to handle. It is not uncommon for homeowners to find themselves in a stare-down with a raccoon over a bowl of pet food. Under normal circumstances, the raccoon is not an aggressive animal and almost always gives a warning prior to attacking. If the threat goes away, the raccoon usually just goes on about its business. When threatened, the raccoon usually lowers its head, humps its back, and lets out a threatening growl. If the threat continues, the raccoon leaps forward with a loud barking sound. If this doesn't deter the threat, the raccoon attacks and bites.

## Intake

One of the most difficult parts of rehabbing raccoons is getting them to hold still. Although often challenging, raccoons need the same intake evaluation and medical documentation as all other rehabilitation animals: do a general assessment, warm the animal, do an initial exam, begin a medical record, and obtain vitals.

Raccoons are animals unlike any other. They can be (and usually are) little bandits and little devils. Although fun to rehabilitate, they must be watched constantly. It is said that if you want to test the integrity of a cage, put a coon in it; if the coon does not get away, it will hold any animal.

## Weight

Raccoons usually weigh from 50 to 70 grams when they come in as newborns. At four weeks they will typically weigh about 400 grams. Raccoons grow quickly and can easily double in weight each week.

Before attempting to rehabilitate them you must get an accurate weight. The only good way to monitor how well babies are progressing is by watching their weight on a regular basis. It's easy to measure their weight change on a two-day (every other day) weighing schedule. Once an animal enters rehabilitation, its weight should consistently increase. A decrease in weight is an indication that something is wrong.

Raccoons will overeat to the point they bloat so care must be taken to monitor all intake. The main indicator that a raccoon is overeating, besides an unreasonable weight gain, is diarrhea. If the animal gets diarrhea, cut back on the quantity of food and things should return to normal within a few days. Another cause of diarrhea is the presence of internal parasites, specifically the raccoon roundworm. Almost all raccoons, even young juveniles, carry roundworms. For this reason, raccoons should be wormed at least once every two weeks with either Strongid® or ivermectin.

### Temperature

A raccoon's normal body temperature is typically between 100.5° and 101.5°F. However, the body temperature of raccoons seems to vary from day to day, unlike most small mammals. For this reason we usually expand the range of what is considered normal to 99.0° to 102.5°F.

### Hydration

Hydration needs to be monitored closely on raccoons because they are always very active and burn a lot of calories. Because of their larger size, raccoons are usually hydrated SQ with lactated Ringer's (see Hydration in Chapter One – Deer).

### Feeding

Newborn raccoons are fragile when it comes to diet. They *cannot* tolerate cow's milk. There are several milk replacement products available. The one we recommend for baby raccoons is KMR® (Kitten Milk Replacer) because of its higher fat content.

It is important not to overfeed the babies. You can feed the infant between 5 and 7 percent of its body weight every four hours. If the animal shows signs of diarrhea, you should cut back on the amount fed. We feed newborns about 5 to 10cc per feeding, five times a day. When they are about four to six weeks old, we increase the feed to 18 to 20cc per feeding, three times a day. Since raccoons are known to overeat, we always monitor and look for any distention of the stomach during feeding. If the raccoon has a full tummy, it's had enough for that feeding.

Until the babies open their eyes, they should be fed KMR® mixed with water at a ratio of one part KMR® to two parts water. After their eyes are open, you can change the formula to one part KMR®, one part baby cereal, and two parts water. The formula should be given at 90 to 100°F and can be delivered using an eyedropper or a syringe with a pet nipple. When the babies get to about 600 grams in weight, you can begin using a regular baby bottle.

Baby raccoons with a surrogate mom.

When feeding, take extreme care to ensure that the mixed formula is not delivered too quickly. Watch for any sign of bubbles coming out the nostrils. If this occurs, it is an indication that the baby is taking too much, too fast. Stop feeding, wipe the nose, and change to either a smaller nipple or a nipple with a smaller hole. If you do not make a change, the baby will aspirate the formula, usually resulting in pneumonia and death. Also, watch that the animal's abdomen does not become tight and distended. If this happens, you are feeding too much. Baby raccoons will overeat to the point of death! It is always better to under-feed than over-feed.

Baby raccoons must be stimulated after feeding so they eliminate urine and fecal matter. This is done by gently rubbing the animal's anus with a warm damp cloth. The stool should be firm to soft and yellowish in color while the baby is on formula. If the animal does not respond to gentle stimulation, try again at the next feeding.

## Weaning

Weaning should start at about eight weeks and the animal should be fully weaned by ten weeks. Raccoons are easy to wean because they will eat and enjoy just about any food offered. As they grow, you can start adding applesauce and puppy chow to the formula, thickening the mixture. The thicker mixture can be given to the babies in a bowl. The feeding goal is eventually to get the raccoon on dry, solid foods.

## Imprinting

There are probably more young raccoons kept as pets than any other wild animal. This is because raccoons seem like they are born already imprinted. Baby raccoons love to be around people. People who feed them are even more popular. A raccoon will behave very similar to a puppy. They like to play, sit on you, wrestle, and just hang out with their people. Raccoons will sleep with you on your bed and they do not need cages. (Note that they like to get into mischief and can cause considerable damage, but they don't *need* to be caged.)

This friendly, pet-like behavior continues until the raccoon reaches four to five months of age. When maturity hits, behavior changes as quick as the click of a switch. The animal will suddenly become mean, vicious, and dangerous. One day you can be happily playing with your pet raccoon and the very next day he will deliver a severe bite.

We refer to this behavior as "reverse imprinting." This is the only animal that we are aware of that reverts back to being wild without any warning. You don't have to look too hard to find someone who at some time had a pet *baby* raccoon, but you will have to search much longer for someone who has had an adult raccoon as a pet.

## Relocation

Raccoons are adaptable and robust animals and are, therefore, easy to relocate. As mentioned previously, they prefer mature woodlands and thrive along streams, lakes, and seashores. They have adapted to

Baby raccoon just hanging out.

almost every major habitat throughout the United States. The best relocation sites for raccoons are habitats that have an abundance of food and water and are far away from people. Raccoons feed on fruit, animal matter, crayfish, insects, acorns, eggs, and sometimes roots.

**The Kill Cage**

Before releasing raccoons, they must be trained to hunt and kill their food. To conduct this training, you will need a "kill cage." This is a large enclosure with a natural raccoon habitat including a pool of water, since raccoons are both land and water hunters. It should be at least 4 feet by 8 feet and be wired in a manner that makes it able to contain mice.

To train the coons, put a few crayfish in the water pool and release a few mice into the cage. Place the raccoon to be tested in the cage and observe it. It should be able to easily catch both crayfish and mice and consume them. If it is unable to successfully hunt and kill, return it to its rehab habitat and increase its offerings of crayfish and mice. Continue to test the animal until it is an "easy hunter."

## Diseases in Raccoons

### Rabies

Raccoons have the reputation of carrying rabies, and it is true that a large number of raccoons do so. Because raccoons are social animals and live in groups, cross-infection between animals is much more prevalent. Raccoons account for more rabies cases in the eastern United States than any other animal except bats. See Rabies in Chapter Two – Skunks.

### Raccoon Roundworm *(Baylisascaris procyonis)*

Found primarily in raccoons, "larval migrans" is the disease process started by the ingestion of the eggs of the raccoon roundworm, *Baylisascaris procyonis.* It involves the prolonged migration and persistence of the larval parasite in internal organs and tissues.

*Baylisascaris* adults reside in the small intestine of raccoons, causing disease primarily in heavily parasitized young raccoons. The adult worms produce and shed eggs in the feces. Adults are known to shed up to six million eggs per day. These become infective in three to four weeks under most environmental conditions. In the Midwest, studies indicate that 70 to 85 percent of raccoons are infected. Due to high population densities of raccoons and the persistence of eggs to live for months to years, the potential for human exposure is high. Animal handlers and rehabilitators are at high risk for exposure.

The most common manifestations of *Baylisascaris* are minor tissue damage and large numbers of parasites; however, *Baylisascaris* can lead to more serious symptoms, including fever, blood disorders, and lung conditions similar to pneumonia. Most seriously, central nervous system (CNS) disease is possible. *Baylisascaris* can develop in the tissues of the nervous system, in particular, the brain. CNS disease depends on the number of larvae entering the brain, their location and extent of migration, and the size of the brain. Progressive CNS disease has resulted in the deaths of at least two children who ingested large numbers of larvae. Ocular larva migrans results when larvae are delivered to the eye by the systemic circulation. Migration of larvae in the retina can cause loss of vision or acute sensitivity to light. Fortunately, human cases of *Baylisascaris* are very rare.

The key to preventing exposure is to reduce contact with feces or areas where fecal matter has lain. The eggs are highly resistant to environmental and chemical disinfectants and can remain adhering to surfaces and dormant in soil for long periods of time.

Cages, traps and rehabilitation areas are sources of contamination and should be handled cautiously. Gloves should always be worn when cleaning or working around contamination sources. Traps and cages should be regularly cleaned and disinfected using a 1:10 mixture of Clorox and water. While not destroying the eggs, this will help remove the protein coat, which makes them sticky enough to adhere to most surfaces. The only accepted method of killing the eggs is through the use of a blowtorch. Propane weed burners work well. When cleaning with a power washer, a face shield should be used to prevent blowback contamination.

### Leptospirosis *(Leptospira interrogans)*

Like skunks, raccoons can shed leptospires in their urine for up to 300 days. Avoiding exposure to the urine of raccoons, either in handling them or coming into contact with places where they have urinated, is the primary course of protection. Protective clothes, boots, and gloves are recommended. Good personal hygiene following any potential exposure is important. See Leptospirosis in Chapter Two – Skunks.

## Coexisting with Raccoons

Raccoons are one of the most common and abundant backyard pests in the United States. They are persistent, curious, and bold animals. Like most other backyard pests, they are constantly on the lookout for food, water, and shelter. The best way to coexist with these animals is to remove from your property the things they want. At night, bring in pet food and bird feeders, empty birdbaths, clean up fallen fruit, and secure trash cans. Remember, the raccoons did not select your property because they either like or dislike you personally, because:

If he can see it, it's his.
If he can smell it, it's his.
If he can hear it, it's his.
If he can touch it, it's his.
If he can't touch it, it's his.
If he wants it, it's his.
and
If it's yours, it's his.

**Coyotes at a Glance**

| | |
|---|---|
| Gestation Period | 62 days |
| Weight at birth | 240 to 275 grams |
| Formula | A mix of Esbilac® and Multi-Milk® |
| Frequency of feeding babies | 4 to 5 times a day |
| Weaned | 8 to 9 weeks |
| Reproduction | Once a year |
| Litter size | 4 to 8 |
| Adult weight | 20 to 35 pounds |
| Hibernation | No |
| Natural foods | Fruits, rodents, rabbits, birds, sheep, carrion, bugs, an occasional deer, pets, pet food, human garbage |
| Normal temperature | 100° to 103°F |

Chapter Four

# Coyotes

## Introduction

Humans have been trying to control coyotes for hundreds of years with little success. They are one of the few wild animals that survive better around humans than they do in undeveloped areas. As we gobble up wildlife habitat, many species suffer. The coyote, however, increases in population and thrives.

Coyotes are misunderstood animals, not well liked, and can be a major nuisance.

In the 1800s, coyotes were found only in the western United States. In the 1940s, coyotes were spotted in New York and are now present in every state and throughout most of Central and North America as well. Coyotes are adaptable animals that live in a wide variety of climates and conditions and adapt to man as well as any animal known. In fact, experts report that coyotes survive better in close proximity to humans' neighborhoods than they do in sparsely populated areas. They are known for killing sheep and raiding chicken coops and rabbit hutches, which makes them unpopular with farmers and ranchers. When humans expand into the coyotes' territory, they also kill house pets, which adds to their unpopular status.

Coyotes have been around for millions of years. They are omnivorous and can adapt their feeding habits to many foods that are available. They usually feed at night or in early morning. Their typical diet consists of fruits, rodents, rabbits, birds, sheep, carrion, bugs, an occasional deer, pets, pet food, and human garbage. Coyotes compete for food with foxes and bobcats, which can have an effect on their population. They are important in the control of rodents, preying on rats, mice, gophers, and squirrels.

Coyotes weigh 20 to 35 pounds and can run up to 45 miles per hour for short distances, making them formidable hunters. They are normally solitary hunters but, on occasion, hunt in pairs and, less often, in packs. The coyote has an established feeding route that it uses daily and ranges up to 100 miles, depending on the availability of food and on the coyote population. Their normal feeding range is from less than one square mile up to as many as 40 square miles.

Although it is not fully documented, many scientists believe coyotes mate for life, and it is not uncommon to see the male helping to care for and feed the pups. Coyotes mate between January and March, have a gestation period of sixty-two days, and produce a litter of four to eight pups once per year. The mother nurses the pups in the den for about six weeks. The male stays near the den while the pups are nursing. The pups will be independent by eight months and most will begin to wander, becoming transients when they are about a year old. They can breed at one year of age, but usually wait until their second year.

In the winter, coyote families usually disperse. Some pups stay in the territory and become transients, and others find new territories and seek out mates to form alpha pairs. Coyotes live from eight to ten years and, like wolves, have been known to mate with domestic dogs. In late winter, the alpha pair mates and begins seeking a den site. They often use the same den each year but the female may dig a new den or several new ones. Coyotes use a den only when they have their young. The rest of the year they sleep on open ground in places known as "lays," or they sometimes seek shelter by digging "weather dens."

Once an alpha pair forms, the animals establish a territory that encompasses their regular hunting area. They sometimes tolerate territory trespass by younger animals but normally defend their territory fiercely.

Coyotes often stay in pairs or alone in their territory. If the pups stay with the mating pair to form a pack, the grown offspring become beta animals and seldom reproduce. All animals in a pack are family members.

Inside their territory, coyotes have what's called a "core area." This core area is intensely guarded and encompasses about 7 percent of their entire territory. The pair spends about 80 percent of their time in the core area. The den is always located in the core area. Coyotes will not allow intruders in the core area or near the den. While mom takes up a position in the den to protect it, the male threatens intruders and will fight to the death to protect his territory.

Coyotes are often found in areas of high human population. Humans provide a wealth of food and a variety of shelter options. Many people think coyotes hunt in packs and are extremely dangerous animals. This is not true. Coyotes are wild animals and, like any other wild animal, can pose a threat. However, they soon learn that, in general, people pose little threat and the animals become unafraid. Being unafraid and being aggressive are clearly different. It cannot be denied that there have been reports of people, usually children, having been injured by coyotes. What is not clear is how the frequency of coyote incidents compares to incidents involving other animals, especially domestic dogs.

## Controlling Coyote Populations

Studies show that attempts to control and reduce coyote populations have been ongoing for hundreds of years. Trapping, den hunting, helicopter hunting, poisons, and artificial birth control are just a few of the methods tried.

Since the early 1930s, the United States government has led the attempts to reduce coyote populations. Probably the most widely used government control tool was the Coyote-Getter, also known as the Go-Getter. This device, introduced in the 1930s, used a 38-caliber cartridge loaded with cyanide. The device was placed in a bait source, so that when the coyote investigated the bait, the cartridge would fire cyanide into its face and mouth. This device, now known as the M-44, is still available for use on private property. While the federal government developed devices and poisons, many ranchers and individuals began using non-registered poisons like rat poison and anti-freeze.

In the 1940s, the government and ranching community began using a new poison called Compound 1080. This was a very potent and effective poison, but it was not popular with many ranchers because it also killed domestic animals. An animal exposed to 1080 dies a slow and painful death. Many people familiar with the effects of 1080 labeled it the most inhumane poison ever developed.

In 1972, the federal government banned the use of animal poisons on public property.

Even with the massive efforts to try and reduce coyote populations, nothing has had an impact. The U.S. Fish and Wildlife service reported that, between 1937 and 1981, the agency had killed 3,612,220 coyotes, and in 1982, the coyote population in the U.S. was at an all-time high. Mankind continues to lose the battle.

Nature is one of the best controllers of coyote populations. Pups are born in late winter or early spring, before rodents and other foods become available. Many pups die from starvation, disease, and the elements. On average, only two pups from each litter live to see September. This natural phenomenon is often counteracted by the food provided by humans.

Humans can also cause an increase in coyote populations by killing the alpha animals. In a family pack, the adult offspring (beta animals) usually do not reproduce, and they sometimes continue to hunt with the alpha pair. If the alpha female is removed from the pack, the beta animals disperse and begin looking for mates, thus establishing new alpha pairs. Many will establish their territory within the original territory. Studies have shown that when family units break up and new units are formed, the resulting territories are often much smaller than the original territory. The final result is the formation of smaller, closely grouped territories, with more alpha pairs and, ultimately, more pups in the same area.

As mankind continues to move into rural areas, the coyote/human conflicts will continue. Efforts are made every day to remove nuisance coyotes. If history is to be our teacher, it may be time to start looking at new ways to coexist with the coyote.

## Coexisting with Coyotes

Coexisting with wildlife is a concept that is slowly starting to emerge in areas where human and animal habitats significantly overlap. Homeowners in many areas are beginning to landscape to deter nuisance animals and are learning to remove temptation by eliminating food and water from their property. However, human willingness to coexist with coyotes is moving more slowly than it is with many other wildlife species. This is simply because coyotes have a bad reputation: they are viewed as dangerous and unpredictable. It is difficult to find anyone who really understands or likes this species. Some of the farmers and ranchers (especially sheep ranchers) who have suffered financial losses from coyotes may never accept these animals as part of their world. To suggest that these ranchers should coexist with coyotes would be like asking a snake to embrace a mongoose.

In addition, many of today's coyote problems occur in residential neighborhoods. Coyotes coming into yards where children play, pets live, and poultry and rabbits are kept is a serious concern of homeowners. People, perhaps unreasonably, expect all roaming wildlife to be controlled the way most municipalities control roaming domestic dogs.

Coyotes, like many species of wild animals, visit homeowners to find food, water, or shelter. In the case of the coyote, once its feeding territory is established, the animal continues visiting the same property until the food, water, or shelter resource is no longer available. Coyotes also aggressively protect and defend their territory so no other coyotes can cash in on all the goodies. For the property owner, this means that the coyote that is there today is the same animal that was there last week. This fact about coyote behavior provides the property owner an accurate view of the scope of the problem. If the property owner selects the easy fix — killing the offender — what happens next? The territory becomes vacant and another alpha mating pair moves in, perhaps this time with a family pack. History has demonstrated that in areas with good habitat, there is a never-ending supply of coyotes.

Other than killing, the only option would be an attempt to coexist with the coyote. This requires making changes to allow the animal to stick around without causing damage. This effort can be costly, time-consuming, and inconvenient, and the coyote is not going to help or cooperate in any fashion.

To reduce the problem, remove all available food (including pet food and fallen fruit), water (including bird baths and standing water), and shelter from your property. If a pet is at risk, don't let the pet out alone, or secure the property line to make it difficult or even painful for the predator to get to the pet. I use three-strand electric fence around my property that keeps furry predators out. Although coyotes can take livestock at any time of day or night, put livestock in a secure pen impervious to coyotes at night, when attacks are the most common. Build a large dog run with a screen top, or perhaps get a bigger dog to protect pets. In a report by F. Robert Henderson, Kansas State University, it was stated that installing lights in the feed area greatly reduced the damage to livestock.

There are many things that can be done to reduce the threat. The problem probably won't ever be completely eliminated, but could perhaps be made tolerable. However, the issue that continues to encourage the outright killing of all coyotes is the fear of being attacked or having children attacked by wandering coyotes. No one will deny that coyote attacks on humans have occurred. But coyotes, unless they are sick or starving, are not aggressive toward humans and they avoid human contact. Paul Rezendes, in his book *Tracking and the Art of Seeing*, says:

> As of 1989, in all of recorded history, there had been only ten documented cases of human beings having been attacked by coyotes (this includes Canada as well as the United States). In contrast, the Humane Society of the United States reported that from 1979 to 1986, 121 people were killed by domestic dogs in this country, for an average of 15 people per year, and that every year, it estimates, between 1 million and 3 million people are attacked by domestic dogs.

## Rehabilitation

### Intake

The intake protocol for coyotes is generally the same as the intake protocol in Chapter One – Deer. However, there are two unique differences in the coyote protocol. Getting accurate weight for the animal is more important, as is careful monitoring of temperature. This is because coyotes are easy to weigh (because of their small size) and they tend to exhibit consistent weight gain. The other unique factor associated with coyotes, because they are canines, is that the rehabber has access to a broader spectrum of medical data and better access to veterinarian support.

### Weight

A regular weight check should be made on each pup. If the animal is gaining weight on a daily basis, it is probably doing fine. If it loses weight two consecutive days, get help from a veterinarian.

## Temperature

The normal temperature of the coyote is 100° to 103°F. The normal acceptable temperature range (when mitigation is not required) is 98° to 105°F.

## Hydration

Check each incoming animal for hydration using the hydration protocol in Chapter One – Deer. Coyote should be rehydrated using the SQ method with lactated Ringer's.

## Feeding

To successfully rehabilitate coyotes, it is important to know how they develop.

At birth, coyotes weigh from 240 to 275 grams and have a normal body temperature of 100° to 103°F. The mother stays with the litter in a den except when feeding. Pups are born with their eyes closed and are helpless. They stay in the den until they are about three weeks of age, after which time they crawl out of the den and stay outside during the day. As they get older, they remain outside the den, day and night, and they start tagging along with mom.

If nursing pups are held for rehabilitation, they must receive a proper diet. Many inexperienced people want to offer any abandoned baby animal a bowl of warm cow's milk. There are very few wild animals that can tolerate or digest cow's milk, and they usually perish on this diet. Coyote pups, like most wild babies, require a special formula of replacement milk. There is a large selection of dog replacement formula on the market. We have been successful using either Esbilac® or Multi-Milk®. Esbilac® can usually be purchased as a powder at any pet store. Multi-Milk® can usually be obtained from a ranch feed store. Baby coyotes should be fed at three-hour intervals with at least one night feeding.

Nursing coyote pups require stimulation after each feeding to ensure they can urinate and defecate without problem. The mother

Baby coyotes at about twenty-five days old.

accomplishes this task by licking the pups' anuses. The rehabber does it with a warm damp cloth, rubbing gently. If the animal does not respond to stimulus after three feedings, seek professional help from your vet.

## Weaning

Baby coyotes are weaned at about eight to nine weeks. At about six weeks, the diet can be supplemented with a high-protein, high-fat, dry puppy chow in a bowl. At eight to nine weeks, start adding small amounts of fresh, raw, red meat cut in small pieces.

## Imprinting

After rehabilitating a litter of coyotes, many rehabbers believe they are in possession of a bunch of fun little puppies. Coyotes will imprint quickly and will take on many of the personality traits associated with dogs. Coyotes, however, will never tame down and take on the domesticated behavioral traits associated with dogs. A coyote might tame down enough to bond with its caregiver, but will always remain a wild animal and will never develop trust toward a stranger.

The best way to treat a rehabilitating coyote is to avoid contact as much as possible, and don't attempt to play with or make friends with the animal. Simply, without speaking, approach the animal's rehab habitat, give it food, turn and leave. Do not let the animal associate you as a friend. If handled correctly, a coyote will growl and threaten even its caretaker.

## Relocation

Relocating coyotes to a new territory is the most controversial part of live handling and rehabilitating them. The critics claim that relocated coyotes will just move into another human population or die from territorial conflicts. To some extent, this is probably true.

It is known that coyote territories are smaller in areas where abundant food exists, and that coyotes will stay and continue hunting in an area with ample food. Rodent and rabbit populations vary according to the availability of food. If you can locate an area with a high concentration of rodents, a new, relocated coyote may be able to squeak out a living. Also, if the coyote is relocated in an area that supports many rodents, there may not be a reason for the relocated animal to seek out human populations.

Most of the people who have told me that they relocate coyotes say that their relocation decisions are based on the overall coyote population. Their rationale is that if coyotes already live there, it must be a good place. The problem with this logic is that coyotes don't eat coyotes, and coyotes don't like other unrelated coyotes. If proper research were done, the rehabber would know that coyotes are solitary animals and live in private territorial areas. Releasing a coyote into an area already inhabited could cause turf fights and disruption of family units.

Baby Coyotes at about eight weeks old.

Most rehabilitators have at their disposal a hunting pen. This is an enclosure that can hold small rats and mice along with the coyote. Before you can release a coyote back into the wild, you have to make sure the animal is capable of hunting and killing prey. Put the pups, one at a time, into the pen with a coyote's natural prey and watch until the animal demonstrates it can catch dinner. To most coyotes, this comes easily and few have problems. If you do have an animal that will not hunt, start cutting back on the dog food and have the animal spend more time each day in the pen until it gets hungry enough to do its job. If you do not have access to a hunting pen, find a rehabilitator who does. Do not skip this step! For a majority of the animals, it will not make a big difference, but the one or two that can't hunt will face certain death if they are released.

## Diseases in Coyotes

Coyotes carry the same diseases as domestic dogs and can easily contract diseases from dogs. Of particular concern are distemper and parvovirus. These are very contagious diseases that cause huge problems in the dog world. You can ask your vet for vaccines and vaccinate coyotes just like dogs.

Also of concern is rabies, especially since coyotes will stay together in a group for some time, and have habitats very close to human habitats. Although we generally do not recommend vaccinating wild animals for rabies, we do consider the coyote an exception to this recommendation. For more discussion of rabies, see Chapter Two – Skunks.

### Distemper

Distemper is one of the most serious diseases a coyote can get. It is a highly contagious and potentially lethal virus that closely resembles measles in humans. It attacks multiple body systems, resulting in a widespread virus that is difficult to treat.

Distemper can be contracted through direct contact, airborne exposure, or in the birthing process. Once released into the environment, the virus is short-lived but can be shed for months by an infected animal. When an animal contracts distemper, it should be isolated from all other animals.

The common symptoms of distemper in coyotes are watery pus discharge from the eyes, a fever, loss of appetite, coughing, clear nasal discharge, diarrhea, vomiting, and pneumonia. As the disease progresses, it attacks the nervous system resulting in head tilting, circling, paralysis, seizures, convulsions, and death. When these late symptoms appear, the animal usually dies.

There is no cure for this disease. The most you can do is treat the symptoms. If you get a case of distemper in your facility, you must clean every contaminated surface with a 10 percent Clorox solution (one part Clorox to nine parts water). Wash everything that made contact with the infected animal including your transport vehicle, any carriers used, towels, catch poles, and so on.

## Parvovirus

Canine parvovirus is a highly contagious virus that can affect coyotes. Animals that have canine parvovirus infection are often said to have "parvo." The virus affects the animal's gastrointestinal tract; it is spread by direct contact and contact with contaminated feces, kennel surfaces, food and water bowls, and the hands and clothing of people who handle infected animals. It is resistant to heat, cold, humidity, and drying, and can survive in the environment for long periods of time. Even trace amounts of feces from an infected coyote may harbor the virus and infect other animals that come into the infected environment. The virus is readily transmitted from place to place via contaminated cages, shoes, or other objects.

The signs of parvovirus include lethargy; loss of appetite; abdominal pain and bloating; fever or low body temperature (hypothermia); vomiting; and severe, often bloody, diarrhea. Persistent vomiting and diarrhea can cause rapid dehydration, and damage to the intestines and immune system can cause septic shock. Most deaths from parvovirus occur within forty-eight to seventy-two hours following the onset of clinical signs. Untreated animals will usually die.

No specific drug is available that will kill the virus. The only treatment available is to treat the symptoms. Treatment should be started immediately and consists primarily of intensive care efforts to combat dehydration by replacing electrolytes, protein and fluid losses, controlling vomiting and diarrhea, and preventing secondary infections. Sick coyotes should be kept warm and receive good nursing care. With proper treatment, survival rates can approach 90 percent.

Since parvovirus is highly contagious, isolation of infected animals is necessary to minimize spread of infection. Proper cleaning and disinfection of contaminated kennels and other areas where infected coyotes are (or have been) housed is essential to control the spread of parvovirus. Use a 10 percent Clorox solution for cleaning.

## Hepatitis

Chronic active hepatitis is an inflammatory disease of the liver found in coyotes. This name refers to the fact that the disease is a long-term inflammatory condition of the liver and its cells. The inflammation is likely the result of the body's own immune system attacking the liver — in a sense, behaving as if the liver were a transplant that it is trying to reject. Hepatitis is usually spread by animal to animal contact, often through blood.

Clinical signs of disease often begin with poor to no appetite and lethargy. Some cases will have a fever, especially as the disease progresses. In advanced cases, chronic active hepatitis often causes a yellowish tint to the whites of the eye, the skin, and the gums, resulting in a clinical condition known as jaundice. Also in advanced cases, the patient will progress to experiencing diarrhea, vomiting, and dehydration.

Once a coyote is diagnosed with chronic active hepatitis (which usually requires liver testing by a veterinarian) treatment begins with IV fluids to hydrate the patient and support the liver, antibiotics to treat any potential secondary infections, and a steroid to halt and prevent inflammation. If the patient is vomiting, anti-nausea medication is administered by injection.

## Mange

Mange is an inflammatory disease in coyotes caused by various types of mites. When the number of mites inhabiting the hair follicles and skin of the animal become excessive, it can lead to skin lesions, genetic disorders, problems with the immune system, and hair loss. Mange may be localized and affect specific areas of the body, or generalized, where it affects the entire body. If localized, symptoms are usually mild, with lesions occurring in patches, especially on the face, trunk, or legs. If generalized, symptoms will be more widespread and appear across the body. These symptoms include a redness of the skin and the appearance of scales and lesions.

The severity of symptoms depends upon the type of mite. Three species of mites have been identified to cause mange in coyotes. While the mode of transmission is unknown for two of these, it is known that one type, *Demodex canis,* inhabits the skin and hair follicles and may transfer from mother to newborn during nursing. Skin scrapings are used to find and diagnose demodicosis in coyotes.

We have found that the best and easiest treatment for mange is injections of ivermectin.

## Foxes at a Glance

| | |
|---|---|
| Gestation Period | 49 to 58 days |
| Weight at Birth | ~1 lb |
| Formula | Esbalac® |
| Frequency of feeding babies | Every 4 hours, 24 hrs/day |
| Weaned | 50 days |
| Adult weight | 5 to 12 pounds |
| Natural foods | Small rodents, rabbits, game birds, reptiles, invertebrates |
| Normal temperature | 101.7°F |

Chapter Five

# Foxes

## Introduction

The fox is a delightful little animal and a lot of fun to rehabilitate. They are reminiscent of an inquisitive, energetic little puppy. A baby fox can get into almost as much trouble as a baby raccoon.

We have not had as much experience with rehabilitating foxes as we have with other animals. We are therefore not as aware of their idiosyncrasies and specific needs as the other animals in this book. We included this brief chapter to provide some basic background information on this species. For rehabilitation purposes, we recommend using the coyote protocols. The only major difference we have noted in rehab requirements is the fox will imprint much more than the coyote. Be careful not to let the animal's friendly personality cause you to give it too much human attention.

## Red Fox

The red fox is the largest fox species. Their body length is from 54 to 78 inches and their weight is between 5 and 12 pounds. An adult male is about 14 to 20 inches tall at the shoulder. Female foxes are usually smaller and weigh about 20 percent less than the males. The tail of the red fox is usually long; it exceeds half a body length and has a white tip. Red foxes have black pointed ears and long canine teeth. On their underside, the fur is white from the nose to the belly.

Female foxes reach sexual maturity at the age of nine to ten months, thus bearing their first litter at one year of age, while male foxes take a little longer to mature. In captivity, their longevity can be as much as fifteen years, though the average lifespan in the wild is two to four years. The species primarily feeds on small rodents, though it may also target rabbits, game birds, reptiles, invertebrates, and young ungulates. Red foxes readily eat plant material, fruits, and vegetables, and in some areas fruit can amount to 100 percent of their diet in autumn. Although the red fox tends to kill smaller predators, including other fox species, it is vulnerable to attack from larger predators, such as wolves, coyotes, and medium- and large-sized felines. The range of the fox is 200 to 250 acres.

Red fox. Note the white-tipped tail.

Females are called vixens, and young cubs, pups, or kits. The forepaws have five digits, while the hind feet have only four and lack dewclaws. They are very agile, being capable of jumping over two-meter-high fences, and swim well. They trot at a speed of 12 to 30 miles per hour, and have a maximum running speed of 30 miles per hour. Vixens normally have four pairs of teats, though vixens with seven, nine, or ten teats are not uncommon.

Red foxes reproduce once a year in spring. The gestation period lasts forty-nine to fifty-eight days. Though foxes are largely monogamous, DNA evidence from one population indicated large levels of polygyny, incest, and mixed paternity litters. Subordinate vixens may become pregnant, but usually fail to whelp, or have their kits killed postpartum by either the dominant female or other subordinates.

The average litter size consists of two to twelve kits, though litters of up to fifteen kits have occurred. Large litters are typical in areas where fox mortality is high. Kits are born blind, deaf, and toothless, with dark brown fluffy fur. At birth, they weigh 56–110 grams and measure 5.7 inches in body length and 3.0 inches in tail length. At birth, they are short-legged, large-headed, and have broad chests. Mothers remain with the kits for two to three weeks, as they are unable to thermo-regulate. During this period, the fathers or barren vixens feed the mothers. Vixens are very protective of their kits, and have been known to even fight off canines in their defense. If the mother dies before the kits are independent, the father takes over as their provider.

The kits' eyes open after thirteen to fifteen days, during which time their ear canals open and their upper teeth erupt, with the lower teeth emerging three or four days later. Their eyes are initially blue, but change to amber at four to five weeks. Coat color begins to change at three weeks of age, when the black eye streak appears. By one month, red and white patches are apparent on their faces. During this time, their ears become erect and their muzzles elongate. Kits begin to leave their dens and experiment with solid food brought by their parents at the age of three to four weeks. The lactation period lasts six to seven weeks. Their woolly coats begin to show shiny guard hairs after eight weeks. By the age of three to four months, the kits are long-legged, narrow-chested, and sinewy. They reach adult proportions at the age of six or seven months.

Red foxes are nocturnal, and prefer to hunt in the early morning hours before sunrise or late evening. It is uncommon to spot them during the day, but they can be caught sunbathing on roofs of houses or sheds. Although they typically forage alone, they may aggregate in resource-rich environments. When hunting mouse-like prey, they first pinpoint their prey's location by sound, then leap, sailing high above their quarry, steering in mid-air with their tails, before landing on target up to 16 feet away. They typically only feed on carrion in the late evening hours and at night. They are extremely possessive of their food and will defend their catches from even dominant animals. Red foxes may occasionally commit acts of surplus killing; during one breeding season, four foxes were recorded to have killed around two hundred black-headed gulls each, with peaks during dark, windy hours when flying conditions were unfavorable. Losses to poultry and penned game birds can be substantial because of this. Red foxes seem to dislike the taste of moles but will nonetheless catch them alive and present them to their kits as playthings.

### Red Fox at a Glance

| | |
|---|---|
| Gestation Period | 49 to 58 days |
| Size | 5 to 12 pounds |
| Common diseases | Rabies, leptospirosis, tularemia |
| Hibernation | No |
| Reproduction | Once a year in the spring<br>Litter size 2 to 12 |
| Natural Foods | Small rodents, rabbits, game birds, reptiles, invertebrates |
| Predators | Wolves, coyotes, felines |
| Senses | Excellent sight, hearing, and smell |

## Gray Foxes

People tend to confuse the gray fox with the red fox mainly because of the reddish-brown fur over much of the gray fox's body including its ears, neck, chest, feet, and parts of the legs and belly. They are also similar in size. The gray fox, however, has a black-tipped tail.

The technical statistics for the gray and the red foxes are very similar with a few exceptions.

The gray fox is monogamous. It breeds in early March. The gestation period lasts approximately fifty-three days. Litter size ranges from one to seven. The pups do not come out of the den until they are about five weeks old and begin to hunt with their parents at the age of three months. By four months, the kits will have developed their permanent dentition and can easily forage on their own. The family group remains together until the autumn, when the young reach sexual maturity, then they disperse.

Gray fox.

The gray fox is primarily insectivorous and herbivorous. Fruit is an important component of its diet and they eat more vegetable matter than does the red fox.

Adults weigh from 7 to 13 pounds and measure up to 40 inches long including a 12-inch tail. The female is slightly smaller than the male. The gray fox is the only American canid that can climb trees.

### Gray Fox at a Glance

| | |
|---|---|
| Gestation Period | 55 days |
| Size | 5 to 12 pounds |
| Common diseases | Rabies, leptospirosis, tularemia |
| Hibernation | No |
| Reproduction | Once a year in March<br>Litter size 3 to 5 |
| Natural Foods | Insectivorous and herbivorous, mice, rats, rabbits |
| Predators | Owls, coyotes, hawks |
| Senses | Excellent sight, hearing, and smell |

## Rehabilitation

Rehabbing foxes is very much the same as rehabbing coyotes. The same procedures should be utilized. One difference is that foxes mature faster than coyotes and therefore can be weaned several weeks earlier.

At birth, foxes weigh 56 to 110 grams. They are born with their eyes closed and are helpless. They stay in the den until they are about three weeks of age, after which they crawl out of the den and stay outside during the day. Kits require almost constant supervision; when suckling, they require milk at four-hour intervals, day and night. Once weaned, they may become destructive to leather objects, furniture, and electrical cables.

Common members of the Sciuridae family include the eastern gray squirrel, Douglas squirrel, American red squirrel, and Richardson's ground squirrel.

## Squirrels at a Glance

| | |
|---|---|
| Gestation Period | 29 to 65 days, depending on species |
| Weight at Birth | 3 to 5 grams |
| Formula | Multi-Milk® plus cream |
| Frequency of feeding babies | 3x/day |
| Weaned | 30 days |
| Adult weight | ~1 lb |
| Natural foods | Seeds, nuts, acorns, tree buds, berries, leaves, twigs |
| Normal temperature | 98° to 102°F |

Chapter Six

# Squirrels

## Introduction

Squirrels are members of the family Sciuridae, which includes small rodents such as tree squirrels, ground squirrels, chipmunks, flying squirrels, and prairie dogs, among others. A group of squirrels is called a scurry or a dray. Some species can run up to 20 miles per hour. Interestingly, squirrels are immune to rattlesnake venom.

The rehabilitation material in this chapter applies to all the squirrels discussed.

## Prairie Dogs

Named for their bark-like calls and black-tipped tail, black-tailed prairie dogs (*Cynomys ludovicianus*) are small, short-tailed animals with eyes and small ears set far back on their heads. Their light-brown fur blends well with the dirt of their den. Prairie dogs average 14 to 17 inches in length and weigh 1 to 3 pounds. With short, muscular legs and long-nailed toes on their front and hind feet, they are well equipped for a burrowing lifestyle.

Prairie dogs are considered a "keystone" species because their colonies create islands of habitats that benefit approximately 150 other species. They are also a food source for many animals, including coyotes, eagles, badgers, and critically endangered black-footed ferrets. Many species, like black-footed ferrets and tiger salamanders, use prairie dog burrows as homes. Prairie dogs even help aerate and fertilize the soil, allowing a greater diversity of plants to thrive.

Black-tailed prairie dogs mainly consume grasses, sedges, forbs (flowering plants), roots, and seeds, though they are also known to eat insects. Black-tailed prairie dogs once numbered in the hundreds of millions — maybe even over a billion — and were possibly the most abundant mammal in North America. But due to a variety of reasons, their numbers have decreased by over 95 percent. Today, they may number around 10 to 20 million.

Prairie dogs are colonial animals that live in complex networks of tunnels with multiple openings. Colonies are easily identified by the raised burrow entrances that give the diminutive prairie dogs some extra height when acting as sentries and watching for signs of danger.

The tunnels contain separate "rooms" for sleeping, rearing young, storing food, and eliminating waste.

Prairie dogs are very social and live in closely knit family groups called coteries. Coteries usually contain an adult male, one or more adult females, and their young offspring. These coteries are grouped together into wards or neighborhoods, and several wards make up a colony or town.

The primary prairie dog social unit, the coterie, occupies an acre or so of territory with fifty to sixty burrow entrances. Members of a coterie recognize each other with an identifying kiss or sniff. Their cohesiveness is maintained by the cooperative activities of raising young, constructing burrows, grooming, playing, and defending the coterie territory.

The dominant male is typically the most active in the defense of the coterie, patrolling its invisible borders and challenging all comers. Prairie dogs warn of territorial trespassers from adjacent coteries or approaching danger by emitting a series of barks, which sound more like high-pitched squeaks. Specific threats are associated with distinctive vocalization patterns that serve to alert all residents of a town to the common threat.

Prairie dogs build up large stores of body fat to carry them through the fall and winter months. Unlike most other members of their family, black-tailed prairie dogs do not hibernate. They may remain underground for several days during periods of harsh weather, but milder winter conditions allow for towns bustling with activity.

## Prairie Dogs at a Glance

| | |
|---|---|
| Natural Foods | Grasses, sedges, forbs (flowering plants), roots and seeds, insects |
| Territorial | No |
| Range | One acre |
| Hibernation | No |
| Reproduction | Once per year, in April or May |

| | |
|---|---|
| Litter Size | 3 to 4 |
| Leave the nest | 6 weeks |
| Predators | Coyotes, eagles, badgers, black-footed ferret |

## Tree Squirrels

The **eastern gray squirrel** is the most common tree squirrel in urban areas. Its upper parts are gray with a reddish wash in summer; its underparts are whitish. They weigh between 15 and 24 ounces and are 16 to 24 inches in length, half of which is its prominent, bushy tail.

The **Douglas pine squirrel, or chickaree,** measures 10 to 14 inches in length including its tail, and weigh 5 to 10 ounces (150 to 300 grams). Its upper parts are reddish- or brownish-gray, and its underparts are orange to yellowish. The Douglas squirrel is found in stands of fir, pine, cedar, and other conifers.

The **red squirrel** is about the same size as the Douglas squirrel. They have small ear tufts in the winter and often have a black stripe separating the dark upper color from the light belly. The amount of red in their fur varies from rust-colored in winter to grayish-red in summer. They are smaller than both the gray and the fox squirrel, weighing 4 to 8 ounces, and are between 9 and 13 inches in length. Red squirrels prefer coniferous forests, but they also can be found in mixed conifer and hardwood forests or sometimes in hardwood habitats. They do not confine themselves to trees and are commonly found on the ground. Red squirrels are solitary except during copulation. The breeding season is February through September. One to seven young are born in each of the two litters. The young disperse after nine weeks. In areas with prolonged periods of cold weather, red squirrels may construct a winter nest underground, often in or near a food storage site. Tree squirrels feed mostly on plant material, including seeds, nuts, acorns, tree buds, berries, leaves, and twigs. However, they are opportunists and also eat fungi, insects, and occasionally birds' eggs and nestlings. They store food and retrieve it as needed. Hollow trees, stumps, and abandoned animal burrows are used as storage sites; flowerpots, exhaust pipes, and abandoned cars are also used. Tree squirrels construct nursery nests in hollow trees, abandoned woodpecker cavities, and similar hollows. Where these are unavailable, they will build spherical or cup-shaped nests in trees, attics, and nest boxes. An alternate nest may be constructed in a tree for summer use. In urban areas, squirrels mostly nest in buildings and other structures. Nests contain leaves, twigs, shredded bark, mosses, insulation, and other soft material.

Depending on the species, tree squirrels mate from early winter to late spring. One litter of two to four young is produced from March to June. They usually have two litters of two to seven pups, the second born in August or September. At about thirty days of age, the young are fully furred and make short trips out of the nest. At about sixty days of age, they begin eating solid foods and venture to the ground. At about ninety days of age, juvenile squirrels are on their own, sometimes remaining close to the nest until their parents' next breeding period. The second litter may stay with the mother in the nest through the winter until well after the winter courtship season.

In trees, squirrels are relatively safe, except for an occasional owl, goshawk, or human hunter. On the ground, large hawks and owls, domestic cats and dogs, coyotes, and bobcats catch squirrels. Vehicles, disease, and starvation also kill squirrels. Most squirrels die during their first year; if they survive that, they live three to five years.

Tree squirrels have many fascinating behaviors. They don't hibernate, but remain in their nests in cold weather, venturing out to find food they stored nearby. Squirrels are most active at dawn and dusk, but sharp eyes aided by a pair of binoculars can spot them moving among the treetops any hour of the day. On hot days, squirrels are less active and remain motionless on branches to enjoy whatever breeze is available. Home ranges for tree squirrels vary, from a half acre to ten acres. For the eastern gray and eastern fox squirrels living in city parks and suburban yards, home ranges average half an acre.

The hind legs of tree squirrels are double-jointed to help them run up and down trees and other objects. Their front claws are extremely sharp for gripping while climbing and traversing.

### Tree Squirrels at a Glance

| | |
|---|---|
| Natural Foods | Seeds, nuts, acorns, tree buds, berries, leaves, twigs |
| Territorial | No |
| Range | ½ acre to 10 acres |
| Hibernation | No. Feeds year round. |
| Reproduction | Twice a year, spring and fall |
| Litter Size | 2 to 7 pups |
| Leave the nest | 60 days |
| Predators | Large hawks and owls, domestic cats and dogs, coyotes, bobcats, humans |
| Life Span | 4 years; 10 years in captivity |

## Ground Squirrels

Ground squirrels are found in the evergreen forests of North and Central America. They are different from tree squirrels because they run into their burrows formed in the ground when startled, while tree squirrels run up trees as their name implies.

Many different types of ground squirrels are found throughout North America. Their body measures 7 to 8 inches, while their semi-bushy tail adds another 5 to 9 inches of length. Their fur is brownish gray and speckled with off-white along the back; the sides of the head and shoulders are light gray to whitish.

Ground squirrels live in a burrow system where they sleep, rest, rear young, store food, and avoid danger. The burrow openings are about 4 inches in diameter but can vary considerably; often there is more than one opening in a burrow system. The tunnels can be 5 to 35 feet or more in length and can extend 2 to 4 feet below the soil sur-

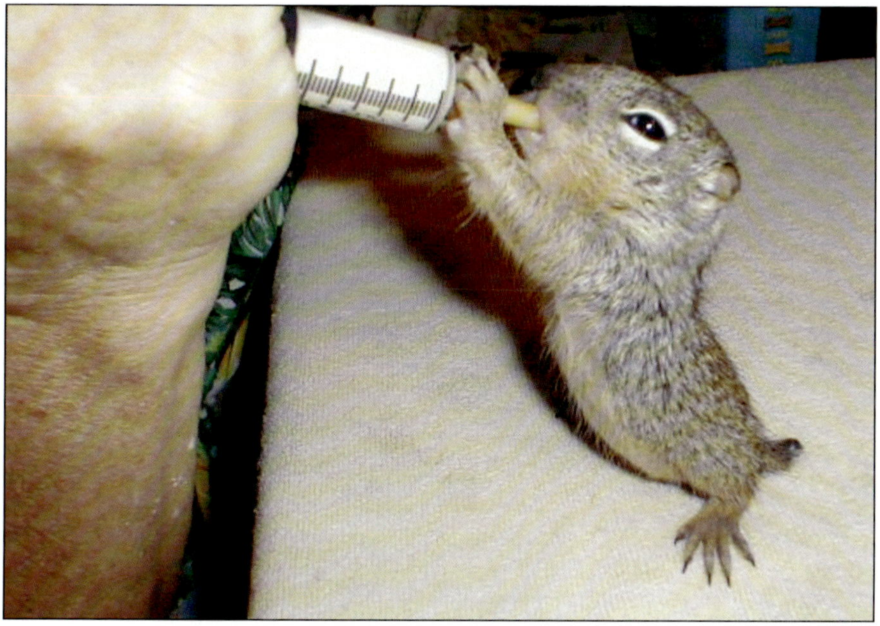

Baby ground squirrel lost his tail.

face. Ground squirrels live in colonies that can include several dozen animals in an underground complex. Their home range typically is within a 75-yard radius of their burrow.

There are three types of burrows: hiding burrows, created for emergency purposes, are short tunnels leading to a dead end and are many in number around the main burrow; nesting burrows are created for females to deliver and raise their litter; and hibernating burrows are used to store food for the winter. These may look similar to the burrows of gophers and moles; however, the ground squirrel doesn't leave any dirt around the entrance. They take the dirt created from the burrowing and pat it down tight with their heads and feet.

Ground squirrels are primarily herbivorous; they eat vegetables, field crops, grasses, seeds, grains, and nuts, and their diet changes with the season. After emerging from hibernation, they feed almost exclusively on green grasses and herbaceous plants. When annual plants begin to dry and produce seed, squirrels switch to seeds, grains, and nuts and begin to store food. They have four front teeth used for cutting and grinding.

Hibernation usually lasts five to six months in the winter, when their body temperature drops to a few degrees higher than the temperature outside. They wake up once a week for about twelve to twenty hours. If the weather doesn't get real cold in the winter, they will skip hibernation.

Ground squirrels breed once a year. Female adult ground squirrels usually deliver seven to eight babies, right after hibernation ends. The young are born in the burrow and grow rapidly. When they are about six weeks old, they usually emerge from the burrow. At six months of age, they resemble adults.

## Ground Squirrels at a Glance

| | |
|---|---|
| Natural Foods | Vegetables, field crops, grasses, herbaceous plants, seeds, grains, nuts |

| | |
|---|---|
| Territorial | No |
| Range | 75 yards |
| Hibernation | Yes |
| Reproduction | Once a year |
| Gestation Period | 30 to 44 days |
| Litter Size | 7 to 8 babies |
| Leave the nest | 6 weeks |
| Predators | Large hawks and owls, domestic cats and dogs, coyotes, bobcats, and humans |

## Chipmunks

There are twenty-three different kinds of chipmunks. They are reddish-brown in color with a single black stripe running down the center of the back. A white stripe between two black stripes runs down each side of its body from the neck to the base of the tail. The chipmunk has a white underside and a white stripe above and below its eyes. They range in size from 8 to 10 inches long (including the tail) and weigh between 2 and 5 ounces. There is no difference in appearance between males and females. They have five toes on their front feet and four toes on their back feet.

Chipmunks are omnivores (they feed on both plants and animals). Their diet includes seeds, nuts, berries, fruits, flowers, mushrooms, insects, worms, snails, frogs, bird eggs, and small birds.

Chipmunks mate twice a year, from February to April and again from June to August. Males and females come together only to mate; females raise their young alone. After a gestation period of thirty-one days, a litter of two to six young is born (although some litters may be as large as nine young). Hairless, blind, and helpless, newborn chipmunks are about the size of a bumblebee. The young remain underground in the burrow for about six weeks. After approximately eight to ten weeks, they are fully independent and leave the mother. They reach sexual maturity in about one year.

### Chipmunks at a Glance

| | |
|---|---|
| Natural Foods | Seeds, nuts, berries, fruits, flowers, mushrooms, insects, worms, snails, frogs, bird eggs, small birds |
| Territorial | Yes |
| Range | ½ acre |
| Hibernation | No |
| Reproduction | Twice a year |
| Gestation Period | 31 days |
| Litter Size | 2 to 6 |
| Leave the nest | 6 weeks |
| Predators | Hawks, snakes, weasels, foxes, bobcats, raccoons, rats, owls, coyotes |

Chipmunks are most active in the early morning and late afternoon. Although they can climb trees, they spend most of their lives on the ground or underground in burrows that may reach 30 feet

An enormous amount of food can be held in a chipmunk's cheek pouches.

long and 3 feet deep. These burrow systems include nesting chambers and storage rooms for nuts and seeds that provide chipmunks with food throughout the winter. The burrow entrance usually measures 2 inches in diameter. Chipmunks remove the fresh dirt from the opening to avoid being conspicuous to predators. They fiercely guard their territory from other individuals. Beginning in late October, chipmunks sleep for long periods throughout the winter but they do not hibernate. They occasionally wake to snack on stored nuts and seeds and may even come outside for brief periods of time on warm winter days.

Chipmunks are very vocal and make a variety of noises. They get their name from the "chip, chip" sound they make. An enormous amount of food can be held in their cheek pouches, which can stretch to three times the size of the head. When gathering large nuts, chipmunks bite off sharp edges and stems.

## Flying Squirrels

The most distinctive characteristics of flying squirrels are the broad webs of skin connecting the fore and hind legs at the wrists, and the distinctly flattened tail. Flying squirrels might more appropriately be called "gliding squirrels," because they aren't capable of true powered flight like a bird or a bat. Flying squirrels glide. When a flying squirrel wants to travel to another tree without touching the ground, it launches itself from a high branch and spreads out its limbs so that the gliding membrane is exposed. It uses slight movements of the legs to steer, and the tail acts as a brake upon reaching its destination. Flying squirrels can cover more than 150 feet in a single glide!

Flying squirrels are smaller than other tree squirrels. They are between 8 and 10 inches in length and weigh between 1.3 and 4 ounces. It can be difficult to distinguish between the two species of flying squirrels because both may be various shades of gray or brown above and lighter below. They are the only squirrels that are active at night and they have very large, round black eyes that help them see.

They are the most carnivorous of all tree squirrels. They eat bird eggs and nestlings, insects, and other animal matter when available. Flying squirrels make their homes in snags, woodpecker holes, nest boxes, and abandoned nests of birds and other squirrels. They often occupy bird houses, especially bluebird houses.

Flying squirrels can have two litters of two to four young each year. The young may stay with the mother through the winter when the squirrels commonly group together.

### Flying Squirrels at a Glance

| | |
|---|---|
| Natural Foods | Nuts, acorns, bird eggs and nestlings, insects, other animal matter |
| Territorial | No |
| Range | ~1 acre |
| Hibernation | No |
| Reproduction | Northern: once a year<br>Southern: twice a year |
| Gestation Period | 40 days |
| Litter Size | 2 to 4 |
| Leave the nest | 6 weeks |
| Predators | Owls, hawks, tree snakes, climbing mammals |

## Rehabilitation

### Intake

Baby squirrels are very small (less than 15 grams) and therefore must be handled with care. They are too small to get a body temperature and too small for a daily weight check, so their overall condition must be accurately noted for monitoring.

Squirrels don't seem to stress as much as many of the other mammals, so they are easier to handle and therefore easier to rehabilitate. Squirrels quickly become attached to their caregivers, thus making them easier to feed and monitor.

They are, however, somewhat difficult to keep warm. External warming is required for babies.

### Weight

Baby squirrels only weigh a few grams at birth, which makes their well-being more difficult to monitor. Because their weight gain is so miniscule, daily weight changes are statistically insignificant. Therefore, with tiny animals, we log weight changes on a weekly rather than a daily basis. This means that special attention must be given to any other physiological changes that occur on a daily basis. As the squirrels get larger, a more frequent weighing program can be initiated. A weight loss over a week's time frame is usually significant and an indication of illness or formula problems.

## Temperature

It is difficult and dangerous to the real small animals to try and get a rectal temperature. Until an animal as small as a squirrel grows big enough to accept a thermometer, we do not monitor temperature.

Baby squirrels should be kept warm, in an aquarium with a heating pad under a small portion of the aquarium. Set the heating pad on low and check it often. It must only be under PART of the aquarium, on the outside, so that the animal can escape to a cooler part of the container if the heating pad setting is too high or it malfunctions.

The aquarium and heating pad should be used on all species of squirrel, but is critical for prairie dogs. Baby prairie dogs have a layer of baby fat and need solid food to maintain this fat. While they are on formula, they can easily lose this insulation, get cold, and die quickly. You MUST use some external heating device with newborn prairie dogs. We often hang an open light bulb over the enclosure in addition to the heating pad.

## Hydration

Because of the location and construction of their nests, abandoned squirrels are often slower leaving their nest in search of mom when she disappears. This fact results in a seemingly larger number of dehydrated animals.

A dehydrated baby will not last long, so keep it full of fluids. If we see an 8 percent or greater loss of skin elasticity, our protocol is to administer a subcutaneous injection of lactated Ringer's solution.

Anything less than 8 percent is treated with oral electrolytes. See Determining Hydration in Chapter One – Deer.

One thing to watch out for in baby squirrels is that after each feeding you must stimulate them to defecate and urinate, otherwise their bladder and bowel will swell up and can even burst. To do this, simply stroke along their tummy towards the anus, which simulates a mother licking and grooming her babies. You can also do this with a warm damp tissue or cloth. The idea isn't to squeeze anything out, just to stimulate the baby to do its business.

## Feeding

At birth, squirrels are hairless and blind, and their ears are closed. Newborns weigh about 10 grams and 84 to 112 grams at five weeks. Young squirrels begin to explore outside the nest about the time they are weaned, at ten to twelve weeks.

Baby squirrels (eight weeks to six months) require a diet higher in protein than adults. The best formula we have found for these animals

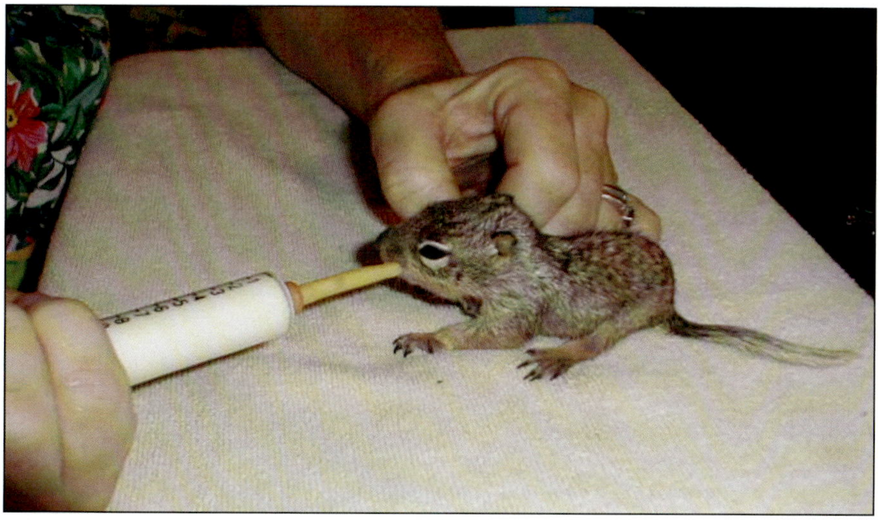

Feeding a rock squirrel with a special nipple.

is Zoologic®. Mix half Gatorade® or Pedialyte® with half Zoologic®; feed the pup SLOWLY, dripping it into the mouth. Be careful that the pup does not gasp and aspirate, which will mean DEATH if the formula gets into the lungs. Take it slow and be patient. Feed a six-ounce baby every two to four hours depending on its condition. Be sure the formula is warm. Putting the baby under your shirt, next to your skin, will help warm it.

You must stimulate the genital area after each feeding in order to help the pup eliminate its waste matter. See detailed instructions above, under Hydration.

Once your baby is ready to take solid foods, offer seeds, nuts, berries, fruits, flowers, mushrooms, insects, worms, snails, and frogs.

### Weaning

Squirrels wean very quickly. At about eight to ten weeks we offer baby squirrels a smorgasbord of treats. We go through our kitchen and get a handful of every cereal, bread, chips, nuts, or any other grain product, shake it up in a dish, and offer it to the babies. They can pick the food of their choice and seem to forget about the milk very quickly.

### Imprinting

Squirrels imprint easily and tend to stay imprinted for life. If, after you release your squirrels, you have one that comes to your feet begging for food, he will approach you for food for the rest of his life. The only thing that you can do to prevent this is to strictly resist undue attention while rehabilitating. Also, keep human contact limited to only one person.

### Relocation

When it's time to relocate the squirrels, the most important thing to remember is to put them away from people and, more importantly, in an area with lots of tree cover and an absence of dogs and cats.

Rehabbed squirrels lose their natural fear more than most animals and therefore make them easy prey for predators.

## Diseases in Squirrels

Squirrels might carry diseases that could affect humans, but, as a practical matter, instances where squirrels have transmitted disease to humans are rare. Any disease, however, transmitted by ticks and fleas can be carried by squirrels. There are very few reported cases of rabies in squirrels.

Occasionally, you may see a tree squirrel engaging in unusual behavior, such as repeatedly falling over or circling a small area. Such behavior can result from an injury, poisoning, or inflammation of the brain (encephalitis) caused by a parasite.

If a person is bitten or scratched by a tree squirrel, immediately flush the wound liberally with tap water, and scrub the wound with soap and water.

### Tularemia *(Francisella tularensis)*

Tularemia (rabbit fever) is caused by the bacterium *Francisella tularensis.* It is carried primarily by rabbits but has also been found in approximately 100 other rodent and squirrel species. It is transmitted through the bite of flies, fleas, ticks, or lice. There are approximately 200 cases of tularemia reported in humans each year, but under-reporting is suspected. Biting flies, ticks, and direct contact with an infected animal are equally responsible as sources of infection. There are two forms of the disease: Type A, which is the more virulent form carried by the vector species, and Type B, a milder form that can be carried by water. Water-borne tularemia predominates in northern regions where muskrat and beavers contaminate surface waters.

After an incubation period of two to ten days, tularemia can take at least four different forms, depending on the method of infection. The most common clinical course is the ulcero-glandular form. At the site of the entry, usually the hands, or at the site of an arthropod bite, a necrotic ulcer develops and the organism spreads to the regional lymph node. Symptoms include chills, high fever, severe headaches, muscle aches, joint pain, nausea, and fatigue. When the organism contaminates the eye, an ulcer often forms on the lower lid. Other forms of the disease include glandular (of the glands; without a skin lesion), typhoidal (post-ingestion), and oropharyngeal. The case fatality rate in untreated cases is 5 to 7 percent. As with other diseases transmitted by tick or insect vectors, handling of animals should be kept to a minimum and gloves should always be worn. It is suggested that any trapped animal be dusted with flea and tick powder prior to being handled.

The family Leporidae includes these North American species:
Eastern cottontail rabbit, pygmy rabbit, marsh rabbit, and desert cottontail.

### Cottontails at a Glance

| | |
|---|---|
| Gestation Period | 49 to 58 days |
| Weight at Birth | ~1 lb |
| Formula | Multi-milk® |
| Frequency of feeding babies | Every 4 hours, 24 hrs/day |
| Weaned | 50 days |
| Reproduction | Up to 12 litters per year |
| Litter size | 2 to 12 |
| Adult weight | 5 to 12 pounds |
| Hibernation | No |
| Natural foods | Small rodents, rabbits, game birds, reptiles, invertebrates |
| Normal temperature | 101.7°F |

Chapter Seven

# Cottontail Rabbits

## Introduction

There are probably more people willing to rehabilitate cottontail rabbits than any other wild animal. Rabbits are cute, fuzzy, quiet, and clean little animals that cause homeowners little concern, as they do not interfere with pets or garbage. Gardeners are the obvious exception to wanting to live around rabbits. Rabbits will eat almost anything green and can eat a lot of it.

Rabbits are also unique in the animal world because their nests are so easily uncovered. People who have pets or children and see a cottontail on their property have a high likelihood of finding a nest of babies.

*Cottontail rabbits cannot be domesticated and do not make good pets. Attempts to keep a wild rabbit in captivity will almost certainly lead to the animal's death.*

These animals can be found throughout the United States and in much of Canada and Mexico. They tend to be social animals and group together in colonies. Their presence is determined by food availability. Cottontails thrive on most plant life and prefer grasses, hay, alfalfa, and garden goodies. They feed from daylight to dusk and are especially active when the grass has dew on it; this is how they get most of their water.

Cottontails breed year-round and can have up to twelve litters per year. The gestation period is twenty-eight days, and the litters range in size from two to twelve. If all the babies, or kits, survived and the population went entirely unchecked, a single mating pair would have a family of over 350,000 in five years. In fact, only about two kits from every litter will ever see adulthood, and the average life span for these rabbits is less than two years.

A cottontail's body temperature is between 101° and 103°F. Cottontails regulate their body temperature by expelling heat from the small blood vessels in their ears. They have keen senses of hearing, smell, and taste, but their eyesight is only marginal. Rabbits are good swimmers and diggers and can climb trees, although they seldom do. They have a very high metabolic rate, about three times that of dogs and cats.

Unlike some other rabbit species that dig and live in burrows, cottontails make their nest by carving out a bowl-shaped depression in the ground in high grass or brush. The depression is about 7 inches in diameter and up to 5 inches deep. It is lined with dried leaves and grass and belly hair from mom. The kits are born hairless, eyes closed, and are totally helpless. Their ears are not fully developed at birth and are pulled back against the side of their head. The kits develop very quickly. At ten days, their eyes and ears open. They begin the weaning process as soon as their eyes open, and they start chewing on the nesting material.

The mother rabbit does not stay with the nest, therefore she does not attract predators. She returns to the nest and nurses the babies twice a day, usually at dawn and dusk. The remainder of the time, she remains hidden in the brush, always keeping a watchful eye on her young. Her primary defense, like that of all cottontails, is to stand completely motionless until danger moves away.

In preparing for feeding, the mother approaches the nest, removes the covering material and lies down on the litter. The babies don't suckle but rather open their mouths and throats, so that the milk runs directly into their stomach. After feeding, mom stimulates each baby

At ten days, these rabbits are starting to open their eyes.

to induce defecation and urination. She does this by licking the baby's anus. This entire process usually takes less than thirty seconds.

At between three and five weeks, the kits will be out of the nest and feeding on their own. They are sexually mature and ready to mate between four and six months of age.

Most gardeners who have bunnies want to get rid of them. This is understandable, because rabbits eat from dawn to dusk and cause a lot of damage. Prior to going after that pesky little rabbit, however, you need to make sure a rabbit is the cause of the damage you are experiencing, because there are many creatures that can cause havoc with trees and gardens.

Examine the plants that have been eaten. A rabbit has sharp, scissor-like teeth and makes clean cuts just above ground level. If the damage is under the soil level or high on the plant, the culprit probably is not a rabbit. Also look for droppings around the damaged area. Rabbit droppings are pea-sized pellets, brown in color, and usually distributed in a small loose pile. If you have damaged trees, look at the chewing pattern. Rabbits generally eat a small patch of bark close to the ground.

If the chewing extends around the tree, it is probably caused by something other than a rabbit.

## Rescuing Baby Cottontails

Each year thousands of abandoned rabbits are rescued from nests. Also, thousands are rescued that don't actually need rescuing.

Cottontails build shallow nests and often place them in yards and gardens. The mother rabbit does not stay with the nest, leaving it unattended for much of the day. Because the nests are shallow, lawnmowers, dogs, cats, and small children can easily uncover them. Once it is uncovered, most people will assume the nest is abandoned and will "rescue" the bunnies inside. Once the little guys are taken from the nest, however, their chance for survival drops drastically.

Before removing the babies from the nest, take time to observe their behavior. If the babies have been abandoned, they will bounce around like popcorn. They will be squeaking and crawling around in search of mom. If they don't exhibit these behaviors, place them back in the nest, and cover it with the original nesting material. Even if the kits have been handled by humans, mother rabbits will not abandon their offspring.

Remember, under normal conditions, mom spends only about sixty seconds a day with the nest. You can continue to check the nest every twelve to twenty-four hours. You can also place a ring of flour around the nest and check for signs of mom coming back to it. If the babies become distressed and need rescue, they will let you know. If mom feels the nest site has been fully compromised, she will move the kits to another location.

If the kits are dislodged from their nest by another animal, you will need to carefully inspect each rabbit for puncture wounds or other trauma. A licensed rehabber or a vet must treat cat-bitten rabbits, with puncture wounds, immediately. If there are no obvious signs of trauma, put the little guys back in the nest and cover it. Keep an eye on the nest, and watch for signs of distress.

If the little ones are fussing and popping around, they probably need rescuing. Pick them up, and immediately put them in a small box (a shoe box is ideal) with their nesting materials. Be aware that even baby bunnies can have fleas and ticks and should be handled with caution.

Baby cottontails are probably the most difficult animals in the world to keep alive after rescuing. Very few inexperienced rehabbers will achieve success with these babies.

## Rescuing Adult Cottontails

Adult cottontails needing rescue are usually suffering from trauma as a result of being hit by a car or caught by another animal. Cottontails are very fragile animals and react poorly to stress. The first thing that should always be done for an injured bunny, adult or baby, is to stabilize it by getting it warm in a quiet, dark environment. Unless its injuries are acute and necessitate immediate care, do not attempt to help the animal until it is stable.

## Rehabilitation

### Intake

Cottontails are fragile and difficult to rehabilitate. They react poorly to stress, and also, they are born with a delicate intestinal-flora balance. They have a weak immune system and can get infections easily, so it's important to keep an ultraclean environment for them. Rabbits seem to do best in a sterile or semi-sterile environment.

Open wounds need to be cleaned thoroughly and disinfected. Small wounds can be treated with Neosporin® or similar antibacterial ointment. Serious open wounds will require professional help.

If another animal has injured the rabbit, it will need immediate medical attention. This is especially true if it has been caught by a cat. A cat bite will contain bacteria that break down cellular material and cause almost immediate infection. If not treated immediately, the rabbit will usually die in a few hours.

Rabbits suffering from an animal bite need antibiotics. Rabbits should not be given any of the penicillin-class drugs. We recommend administering either Bactrim® (trimethaprim/sulfa) or Batril® (enrofloxacin), orally or by injection. Dosage depends on the animal's weight and can be determined by your veterinarian.

## Weight

The best way to determine how the animal is progressing in its recovery is by monitoring its weight. Like the squirrel, these animals are so small (only a few grams) that you should monitor weight changes on a weekly rather than a daily basis. You should see a weekly weight gain or at least a weight that remains constant.

## Hydration

Check the rabbit for hydration by pinching the skin on its back and observing how fast the skin returns to its original position. If the skin tends to remain pinched after you let it go, the animal is dehydrated. If this is the case, begin the rehydration process before continuing treatment (see Determining Hydration, Chapter One – Deer). Try to give the rabbit several milliliters of electrolytes orally, every hour.

## Feeding

Most mammals receive colostrum from their mother's milk in the first few hours of life. The colostrum allows the baby to develop a strong immune system. Rabbit babies do not get colostrum. Fatty acids in the mother's milk actually produce a sterile stomach and intestinal tract in the kits. The lack of intestinal flora makes the animals very susceptible to pathogenic bacteria and toxins, which usually cause death. This buildup of internal toxins can be intensified by stress. Stress can result from a variety of external stimuli, including contact with humans, a change in diet, or a change in environment. The normal sign of flora imbalance and stress is diarrhea, but a patient can appear to be totally healthy and active and then drop dead an hour later with no signs or warning.

To help prevent infections, it is recommended that only one person handle the animals, and handling time should be kept to a minimum. All feeding tools should be boiled after each feeding and kept sterile.

## Coprophagy

Adult cottontails engage in coprophagy, which is the ingestion of a fecal discharge. These feces are soft, mucous-covered material that is usually excreted by the rabbit at night. They are called cecotropes, and they contain a highly concentrated vitamin B and mineral supplement that is manufactured in the digestive tract. Rabbits usually ingest this material directly from the anus as it is produced. After ingestion, the cecotropes mix with partially digested food in the cecum and provide nutrients. The material is then expelled in the form of dryer pellets that are widely recognized as normal rabbit excrement.

It has been demonstrated that cecotropes help balance the gut flora and significantly strengthen the immune system of baby bunnies if administered prior to giving the baby solid foods. To provide this material to babies, rehabbers must collect cecotropes from adult rabbits.

## Collecting Cecotropes

All rabbits, male and female, wild and domestic, produce cecotropes. Therefore, to collect cecotropes, any rabbit will do. You will need a cage with a raised wire floor to allow the pellets to fall through. You also will need an Elizabethan collar that snugly fits the rabbit.

Place a newspaper under the wire floor of the cage to act as a catch basin for the cecotropes. Put the collared rabbit in the cage overnight. In the morning, you should have several mucous-covered pellets that can be used to supplement the kits' diet.

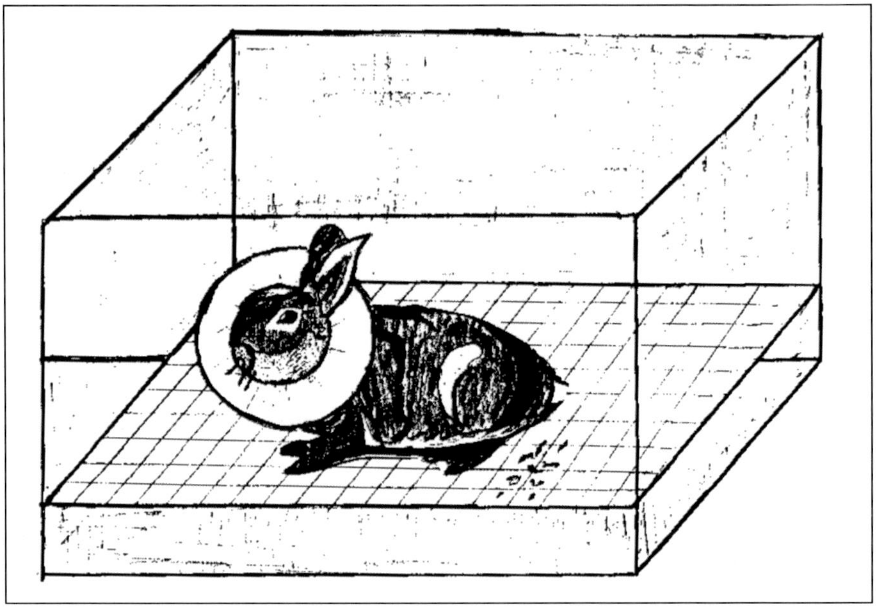

Collection cage for capturing cecotropes.

The collected cecotropes can be pulverized into a thick paste, which can then be thinned with sterile water and made ready to add to the baby's formula. Excess cecotropes can be placed in the freezer. They will remain usable for several months.

**Formula**

Rabbit milk is very high in fat content. Most of the common animal replacement formulas like Esbilac® and KMR® will not provide the proper nutrition to baby bunnies. However, these replacement products will work if they are mixed with high-fat cream in a ratio of three parts replacement milk to one half part cream [3:0.5].

Add one drop of the cecotrope solution for each rabbit at one feeding per day. For example, if you mix enough formula to feed six rabbits, add six drops of cecotropes.

The first feeding of baby rabbits should consist of electrolytes only, to help ensure the animals are properly hydrated. Pedialyte® is an excellent choice and can be purchased at any drug store. The next three or four feedings should be a mix of three parts formula to one part Pedialyte®. For the next three to four additional feedings, continue to increase the proportion of formula until you are feeding 100 percent formula.

Baby bunnies should be fed twice a day, once in the morning and again in the evening. The formula should be warm (not hot) and administered with a small syringe without a needle. The babies may not suck on the syringe, but will drink if the formula is slowly dripped into their mouths. Most babies will eat between 1ml and 3ml of formula per feeding.

Feed the infant until its tummy looks full, but don't allow it to continue eating until the stomach bulges. Overeating can kill the rabbit. While feeding, if you see bubbles coming out of the nose, stop feeding immediately. This is a sign that the bunny is aspirating the food, which can also be lethal. After each feeding, you must stimulate the baby to urinate and defecate. You can use a warm damp cloth and rub the anus very gently. If the kit does not respond to this stimulus, seek help from a licensed rehabber. Stimulation is no longer required after the rabbit's eyes open.

## Weaning

Cottontails develop very quickly and can be weaned in about two weeks.

Because of their delicate digestive system, they tend to get into trouble when the weaning process begins and they start receiving greens. To help prevent contamination, you should wash all food offered to rabbits.

## Imprinting

Rabbits do not seem to imprint on their caretakers. They are not social, nor are they in any way aggressive. *They do not make good pets and will often pass away if kept in captivity after they are weaned.*

### Relocation

We have discovered that the sooner rabbits are released, the better their chances of survival. We recommend that bunnies be released as soon as they are consistently eating solid foods. This usually occurs when they are about the size of a tennis ball. Cottontails are not territorial animals, so they can be released in any location where cottontails are known to live.

## Diseases in Cottontails

Rabbits can be carriers of any tick-borne disease, primarily tularemia (see Chapter Six – Squirrels) and Rocky Mountain spotted fever.

### Rocky Mountain Spotted Fever

Rocky Mountain spotted fever (tick fever) is the second most common tick-borne disease in the United States and is caused when a human is infected by rickettsias. Rickettsias are tiny organisms between viruses and bacteria in size. Rickettsias are unable to reproduce unless attached to a host. The disease is transmitted from a reservoir rodent to a human via ticks. The tick bites the rodent, acquiring the rickettsias, then bites the human, transmitting them into the blood stream. Carried on rabbits, rodents, and the Virginia opossum, the American dog tick in the east and the American wood tick in the west are the regional primary vectors.

Human infection is characterized by a three- to fourteen-day incubation period followed by non-specific signs of the disease such as lethargy and weakness, rapidly progressing to fever, chills, headache, muscle pain, and pain in the joints. Fever is the most predictable and persistent sign. In 88 percent of the cases, generalized spotting or blotchiness starts first on the extremities, next on the palms and soles, and then rapidly spreads to the trunk. Pinpoint hemorrhages are common.

In the absence of a diagnosis and specific therapy, a 15 to 20 percent mortality rate results. Even with effective antimicrobial therapy, a 2 percent mortality rate in the US results. Annually, about 50 people die from this disease; 600 to 1,200 cases are reported each year. Early diagnosis and initiation of therapy, before serologic or isolation evidence, leads to a rapid uneventful recovery in most cases.

## Opossums at a Glance

| | |
|---|---|
| Gestation Period | 12 to 13 days |
| Weight at Birth | 2 to 3 grams |
| Formula | Esbilac® (only) |
| Frequency of feeding babies | 5x/day |
| Weaned | 50 days |
| Reproduction | Varies by region: one per year in the north; up to three in the south |
| Litter size | Up to 15 |
| Adult weight | 1 to 3 pounds |
| Hibernation | No |
| Natural foods | Vertebrates, invertebrates, plants, fruits, grains, and carrion |
| Normal temperature | 95°F |

Chapter Eight

# Opossums

## Introduction

Virginia opossums are robust marsupials, with short legs and thick bodies, about the size of a house cat. They are usually solitary animals, staying in one area as long as food and water are easily available. Though they will temporarily occupy other animals' abandoned burrows, they do not dig or put much effort into building their own. Sometimes families will group together in these burrows or even under houses. As nocturnal animals, they favor dark, secure areas, either below ground or above; they also den in trees.

When threatened or harmed, they will "play possum," mimicking the appearance and smell of a gravely ill or dead animal. This physiological response is involuntary, like fainting, rather than a conscious act. In the case of baby opossums, however, the brain does not always react this way at the appropriate moment, and therefore they often fail to "play dead" when threatened. When an opossum is "playing possum," its lips are drawn back, the teeth are bared, saliva foams around the mouth, the eyes close or half-close, and a foul-smelling fluid is secreted from the anal glands. The stiff, curled form can be prodded, turned over, and even carried away without reaction. The animal will

An opossum "playing possum."

typically regain consciousness after a period of a few minutes to up to four hours, a process that begins with slight twitching of the ears.

Their semi-prehensile tails are not strong enough to support a mature adult's weight. Instead, the opossum uses its tail as a brace and a fifth limb when climbing. The tail is occasionally used as a grip to carry bunches of leaves or bedding materials to the nest. Their fore and hind feet have five toes, all with sharp claws except for the clawless, thumb-like, opposable innermost toe on the hind feet. Although they have keen eyesight, their ability to recognize color is limited. They have large delicate ears, which are predominately furless, making frostbite extremely common. Their long tails are also common victims of frostbite.

Threatened opossums (especially males) will growl deeply, raising their pitch as the threat becomes more urgent. Males make a clicking "smack" noise out of the side of their mouths as they wander in search of a mate, and females will sometimes repeat the sound in return. When separated or distressed, baby opossums will make a sneezing noise to signal their mother. If threatened, the baby will open its mouth and quietly hiss until the threat is gone.

Virginia opossums become sexually mature within the first year of their life, around six months for females and eight months for males, but typically begin breeding around ten months of age. This species has a long breeding season. They average only one litter per year, but in warmer climates the number of litters may increase to three per year with up to fifteen babies per litter.

An opossum's hind foot. Note the opposable thumb-like toe.

The offspring (embryos) weigh 0.13 to 0.20 grams and are generally about 14mm long. They are hairless and pink. There are an average of eight pouch-young per litter. They remain in their mother's pouch and attached to the mammae (nipple) for approximately 50 to 70 days. After the period spent within the pouch, the young remain with their mother, either staying in the den while she forages or riding on her back, where they will cling tightly even when she is climbing or running. Most young Virginia opossums become solitary after weaning; however, some may remain with their mother in the den until they are about 120 days old. About 60 percent of the young will not survive once they are fully independent.

Virginia opossums have a fairly short lifespan; wild individuals typically only survive about eighteen months to two years. Most reproductive females are under a year of age, and few live long enough to breed a second year. The oldest documented free-living Virginia opossum was a three-year-old male from Maryland.

Given the frequent urban habitation of Virginia opossums, interaction with humans is almost inevitable. They are often seen a pest species. Stomach content analyses in Portland, Oregon found that as much as 9 percent of an opossum's diet was composed of garbage; like-

When baby opossums leave the den, they usually ride along with mom.

wise, another 9 percent of their diet was pet food. They are also seen as farm pests due to their appetite for poultry and eggs.

Opossums are not picky eaters. As scavenger omnivores, opossums eat everything from last night's meatloaf to grass. Food sources typically include dead animals, berries, and nuts. Opossums will also hunt mice, birds, and chickens. They commonly prey on snakes, including poisonous species, and are immune to pit viper venom. If it's edible and accessible, the opossum will eat it.

## Rehabilitation

### Intake

The standard intake protocols are used with opossums, but keep in mind that possums do not suckle so feeding is more complex and can result in over- or under-feeding.

## Temperature

Like other small mammals, the opossum will come in hairless and with little body weight. Normal body temperature is 95°F. In order to maintain an adequate body temperature, external heat sources should be used, both heating pads and a light bulb.

## Hydration

Babies that are tube-fed are more difficult to keep hydrated. It is suggested that a baby opossum receive a formula that contains one-third electrolyte solution.

## Feeding

Bringing baby opossums into rehab can be challenging. They are tiny, fragile, and not adept at sucking, so feeding is difficult. The industry standard is to provide an animal with 5 to 7 percent of its body weight per feeding. Possums often weigh less than 10g, and 1cc of Esbilac® weighs about 1.1g, which makes measuring and administering formula a very precise operation, especially since feeding must be done with a feeding tube (see Tube Feeding in Chapter One).

While in the mother's pouch and attached to a nipple, the babies don't suckle, but get their milk mostly by gravity. When in the hands of a rehabber, they will lick the feeding implement but usually will not swallow. It is also difficult to determine the quantity of feed to offer these tiny creatures, as discussed above.

To feed the little guys, we use Esbilac® and a size 3.5 feeding tube. We inject 0.5cc of formula and then look at the baby's tummy to determine if there is evidence of a feeding. If not, we inject another 0.5cc. This is the maximum we feed at each feeding. Being marsupials, possums are in the pouch twenty-four hours a day, so we include a night feeding with opossums.

Adult possums, in general, are easier to feed and care for. They are typically good eaters and are not that picky about what they take.

### Weaning

The young begin eating solid food at around 85 days old and are fully weaned between 93 to 105 days old.

Because they start out so small, we don't start weaning them until about thirteen weeks. By that time, the possums are ready to eat hard food and can be weaned with wet dog food followed by dry dog food mixed with baby cereal or applesauce. See more important diet information under Metabolic Bone Disease, below.

### Imprinting

Like most animals, opossums will imprint but like raccoons seem to revert back to the wild with age. They do not revert back as suddenly as raccoons but when they get older they will leave the rehab center if given a chance.

### Relocation

Opossums are such robust animals and have such a varied diet that they can be released almost anywhere. The biggest concern is releasing them too close to civilization. They are known garbage hunters and most homeowners don't want them around.

## Diseases in Opossums

Possums are known to carry fleas and ticks, so any disease spread by fleas and ticks is possibly carried by the possum. The most common tick disease that is spread by the possum is Rocky Mountain spotted fever.

These animals are also known carriers for at least twenty-four internal and thirteen external parasites. Thus it is highly recommended that possums in rehab be treated regularly for parasites.

## Metabolic Bone Disease

One of the biggest concerns when raising possums is metabolic bone disease (MBD). This is common in captive possums and is caused by feeding an incorrect diet, especially when they are very young. It can develop at any stage of their lives, even in an animal as young as a few days old.

MBD results when the animal is fed a diet where the ratio of Vitamin D, calcium, and phosphorus is out of balance. A successful balance is a diet that is twice as high in calcium as it is in phosphorus. A diet too high in phosphorus results in a decreased absorption of calcium, which causes the tissues and organs to calcify, resulting in MBD. Vitamins D, C, E, K, and magnesium also assist in absorbing calcium. Some foods high in phosphorus include fish, meat, cheese, nuts and seeds, and beans. Foods high in calcium include dandelion greens, many leafy greens (not dark leafy greens), oranges, and papaya. Possums should also get a good dose of sunlight on a daily basis. UV lights are also calcium builders.

We recommend Esbilac® for baby possums because it is formulated with a higher calcium content than many other milk replacers. A formula diet of Esbilac® supplemented with a small dose of vitamin E once a week should get the baby to a weaning age successfully. After weaning, take the time to select calcium-rich foods for its diet and your chances of releasing a healthy critter will be good.

MBD in possums is very much like arthritis in humans. The bones get thin and become malformed and brittle; the animal loses its ability to chew and loses use of its tail.

## Rabies

Although they are not immune, it is unusual for this species to be a carrier of the rabies virus.

## Rocky Mountain Spotted Fever

Rocky Mountain spotted fever (tick fever) is the second most common tick-borne disease in the United States and is caused when a human is infected by rickettsias. Rickettsias are tiny organisms between viruses and bacteria in size. Rickettsias are unable to reproduce unless attached to a host. The disease is transmitted from a reservoir rodent to a human via ticks. The tick bites the rodent, acquiring the rickettsias, then bites the human, transmitting them into the blood stream. Carried on rabbits, rodents, and the Virginia opossum, the American dog tick in the east and the American wood tick in the west are the regional primary vectors.

After a human is bitten, there is a delay in the actual transmission of the disease-causing microorganism from the tick to the host. A reactivation process occurs, leading to a four to twenty-hour delay of infection. Human infection is characterized by a three to fourteen day incubation period followed by nonspecific signs of the disease such as lethargy and weakness, rapidly progressing to fever, chills, headache, muscle pain, and pain in the joints. Fever is the most predictable and persistent sign. In 88 percent of the cases, generalized spotting or blotchiness of the skin starts first on the extremities, next on the palms and soles, and then rapidly spreads to the trunk. Pinpoint hemorrhages are common.

In the absence of a diagnosis and specific therapy, a 15 to 20 percent mortality rate results. Even with effective anti-microbial therapy, a 2 percent mortality rate in the U.S. results. Annually, 600 to 1,200 cases are reported and about 50 people die from this disease. Early diagnosis and initiation of therapy, before serologic or isolation evidence, leads to a rapid uneventful recovery in most cases.

# Afterword

The rehabilitation process can best be summed up by the story of Bert the dunderdeer. Bert was a white-tailed deer found walking down a highway late at night. He was only a few days old, scared, confused, and hungry. Luckily, he was found and picked up by a family with two young daughters. The daughters loved Bert and he was pretty fond of them, even though they were dunderheads.

They took Bert home and decided he should be the new family pet. Bert loved this idea. He moved into one of the kids' bedrooms and everything was blissful. He got to eat whenever he wanted, he got to watch TV, he could occasionally play in the bathtub, and all was good.

After a few weeks, the dunderheads found out it was illegal to possess a wild deer and they could be facing a big fine. The decision was tearfully made that Bert had to go.

Bert was turned over to us for rehabilitation. He was a really friendly deer and wanted continuous attention. He wasn't satisfied with deer pellets and corn like the other deer; he wanted carrots, acorns, watermelon, a full variety of fruits, and people food.

Our challenge was to try and get Bert "untamed" enough that he had a chance of release back into the wild at some future date. To help this process along, we put him in a pasture with some really wild deer hoping he would blend in and mimic their behavior.

Bert, all grown up.

We kept Bert for about six months, trying to keep personal interaction to a minimum. This was difficult because he wanted to be right in middle of everything with a person involved.

At release time, we had seven deer plus Bert to relocate. We decided to go ahead and release Bert with the others in hopes that he would join the herd and become a real deer. Things went well for about two weeks before we got the call. There was a deer hanging out at a local convenience store causing problems and the store owner wanted it removed.

When we arrived at the store, we found a deer outside the front door, lying on the sidewalk. The store owner told us the deer had been there for about a week and greeted everyone entering the store. At first he enjoyed the new visitor. However, he told us, the deer was starting to venture into the store and bug the customers. He said that every